Wan Li: Resolute Reformer and Legislator

Ding Longjia & Ye Peng

Published by
ACA Publishing Ltd.
University House
11-13 Lower Grosvenor Place,
London SW1W 0EX, UK
Tel: +44 (0)20 7834 7676
Fax: +44 (0)20 7973 0076
E-mail: info@alaincharlesasia.com
Web:www.alaincharlesasia.com
Beijing Office
Tel: +86(0)10 8472 1250
Fax: +86(0)10 5885 0639

Authors: Ding Longjia & Ye Peng
Editors: Martin Savery and David Lammie
Translator: Jiang Lin
Cover art: Daniel Li

Published by ACA Publishing Ltd in association
with the People's Publishing House

© 2014, by People's Publishing House, Beijing, China
ALL RIGHTS RESERVED. NO PART OF THIS
PUBLICATION MAY BE REPRODUCED IN MATERIAL FORM,
BY ANY MEANS, WHETHER GRAPHIC,
ELECTRONIC, MECHANICAL OR OTHER, INCLUDING
PHOTOCOPYING OR INFORMATION STORAGE, IN WHOLE OR IN PART, AND
MAY NOT BE USED TO PREPARE
OTHER PUBLICATIONS WITHOUT WRITTEN
PERMISSION FROM THE PUBLISHER.

The greatest care has been taken to ensure accuracy but the
publisher can accept no responsibility for errors or omissions, or
for any liability occasioned by relying on its content.

ISBN 978-1-910760-16-1

A catalogue record for *Wan Li: Resolute Reformer and Legislator*
is available from the National Bibliographic Service of the British Library.

Glossary of Terms

CMC	**Central Military Commission**
CPC	**Communist Party of China**
CPG	**central people's government**
CPPCC	**Chinese people's political consultative conference**
KMT	**Kuomintang (Nationalist Party)**
NGO	**non-government organisation**
NPC	**national people's congress**
PLA	**People's Liberation Army**
PRC	**People's Republic of China**
SEZ	**special economic zone**
SOE	**state-owned enterprise**
SDPC	**state development planning commission**
SPC	**state planning commission**
TCM	**traditional Chinese medicine**

Democratic figures/personages refer to people of note who are 'members of non-CPC political parties'

Preface

The reform and opening up of China ushered in the socialist road with Chinese characteristics and sparked the dawn of a new era. The immortal and meritorious services of Deng Xiaoping, the initiator, chief designer and commander-in-chief of that road, will be eternally engraved on the minds of the Chinese people. He accomplished these outstanding feats with his selfless comrades-in-arms and senior army generals blazing a trail, and going through fire and water with him. The founding fathers and commanders-in-chief of the reform and opening up prompted hundreds of millions of Chinese people to embark together on the new journey that we are still following today. Their eminent contributions deserve to be documented and their deeds should be remembered and admired. They are the role models and examples for the broad masses of party members and cadres to follow on the new journey of reform and opening up.

To cherish the memory of these founding fathers of reform and opening up and to enable readers, especially party members and cadres, to know them better and to learn from them as role models, we decided to publish the *Pictorial Biographies of the Founding Fathers of China's Reform and Opening Up* series. To present these books to readers at the earliest opportunity, we will publish this series volume by volume as each book is completed.

China has entered a new era of reform and opening up. The party central committee with comrade Xi Jinping as general secretary has declared the epoch-making new manifesto of reform and opening up. The implementation of the manifesto requires the devotion and joint efforts of brave generals keeping pace with the times, losing no time moving ahead, fearing no upheavals, abolishing outdated laws and regulations, and defying the negative statements of others; it requires innumerable cadres hurling themselves into the reform and opening-up process; and it requires the collective efforts of hundreds of millions of people. Only in this way can our great cause keep on advancing!

People's Publishing House, August 2014

Alain Charles Asia (ACA) Publishing Ltd is delighted to be associated with the People's Publishing House to bring this book to an English-speaking readership.

ACA, formerly known as ACP (Alain Charles Publishing) Ltd Beijing, was founded in October 1989 and was the first foreign-owned publishing company to be allowed to open an office in China.

In 2007, ACP Beijing was renamed ACA Publishing Ltd to better reflect its focus on China and the Asia-Pacific region. The company specialises in publishing books about China for international readers and has offices in Beijing and London.

ACA Publishing Ltd, October 2016

Contents

Preface IV

Chapter 1 Choice of Qufu Second Normal School due to Rmb5 Subsidy 1

Chapter 2 Stifling the December 9th Student Movement 7

Chapter 3 Establishing the CPC Dongping County Work Committee in His Home 12

Chapter 4 'Dongping-Wenshang People's Self-Defense Force' Holds High the Anti-Japanese Banner 20

Chapter 5 Appointed Director of the CPC's Taixi Special Committee Publicity Department 25

Chapter 6 Lufang Breakout Battle Shocks the Nation 30

Chapter 7 Landlady Protects Births of Revolutionaries' Descendants ... 36

Chapter 8 Continuously Implementing a Bold Delegative Leadership Style 40

Chapter 9 Total Support for the Liu-Deng Army 47

Chapter 10 Taking Control of Nanjing and Governing the Southwest ... 53

Chapter 11 Buying White Curtains for His Mother with His Allowances ... 60

Chapter 12 Helping Premier Zhou Build the Great Hall of the People ... 64

Chapter 13 Sending His Eldest Son Wan Bo'ao for 10 Years' Rural Labour 71

Chapter 14 Subjected to Criticism and Struggle with Three Model Workers on New Year's Eve 77

Chapter 15 Blocking His Elder Sister Wan Yun's Promotion 83

Chapter 16 Making a Breakthrough at Xuzhou Railway Bureau 87

Chapter 17	Going to Zhengzhou Railway Bureau Three Times to Tackle Thorny Issues 94
Chapter 18	No Choice But to Sign After Being Singled Out by Hua Guofeng 102
Chapter 19	Thousands of People Petition the Ministry of Railways 108
Chapter 20	Hospitalised for Treatment Due to Continuous Tussles 113
Chapter 21	Cutting Through the Chaos to Solve the Cover-up in Anhui 118
Chapter 22	'Six Articles' Prelude to Rural Reform 125
Chapter 23	Low-Profile, Large-Scale Rural Investigation 134
Chapter 24	Restoring Order Out of Chaos in Early Rural Policy 139
Chapter 25	Biggest Drought in 100 Years Induces 'Lending Land to Survive Famine' 144
Chapter 26	Shannan District, Feixi County Contracts Production to Households 149
Chapter 27	Chuxian Prefecture's Three 'Secret Weapons' 156
Chapter 28	Fengyang Implements 'All-Round Responsibility System' while Xiaogang Contracts Production to Households 162
Chapter 29	Province Approves Shannan Trial to Contract Output to Households 171
Chapter 30	Enormous Pressure from Beijing 179
Chapter 31	Lao Chen, You Have My Approval to Do This for Three to Five Years 185
Chapter 32	Registering for Production Contracted to Each Household ... 190
Chapter 33	Central Committee Issues Document No.75 in 1980 199
Chapter 34	100 Leaders in Charge of Agriculture Investigate the Rural Areas .. 206

Chapter 35 Five Central Committee No.1 Documents Issued in Succession..212

Chapter 36 Three Experiences of Rural Reform..219

Chapter 37 The Important Topic of Political Restructuring......................224

Chapter 38 Accelerating Legislation in the Spirit of Reform....................230

Chapter 39 Suggesting a Modification to the 1982 Constitution..............238

Chapter 40 Not Inquiring into Matters, Running Affairs or Stirring Up Trouble...242

Chapter 41 Honorary Chairman of the Chinese Bridge and Tennis Associations..251

Chapter 42 Still Keeping a Watchful Eye on Socialist Legal Construction..260

Epilogue...265

Chronology..269

Chapter 1

Choice of Qufu Second Normal School Due to Rmb5 Subsidy

On 1 December 1916 Wan Li was born in an impoverished family in Xijuanpeng street, Zhoucheng town, Dongping county, Shandong. With an infant name of Xiufeng, his formal name was Wan Mingli, which was later changed to Wan Li.

Dongping county was close to Dongping lake with a water surface area of 124.3sq km and an average depth of 2.5m. Dongping lake used to be called Liao'er depression, Daye pond, Juye pond, Langshan moor and Anshan lake in ancient times and got its present name in the reign of Xianfeng of the Qing dynasty. It is the only remaining water left over

A panoramic view of the rebuilt former residence of Wan Li

A spectacular view of the beautiful 160,000sq km Dongping lake

from the 160,000sq km Liangshan moor in *The Water Margin* (a classical Chinese novel written in the vernacular, the first of its kind in Chinese history).

The third-born child of his family, Wan Li's father had four brothers and three sisters. Wan Li was the eldest and only son of his family. He had two sisters named Wan Yun and Wan Ling. His elder generation lived in an increasingly worsening financial situation. When Wan Li was less than two years old, his father Wan Jinshan left his home to make a living, joined Yan Xishan's troops in Shanxi and was promoted from the ranks to be a company commander.

A waterside stockade village on the Dongping lake shore

After the Japanese army invaded and occupied Shanxi, in the Zhongtiaoshan combat during the battle of Linfen, Wan Jinshan's troops ran out of ammunition and food supplies after fierce fighting against the Japanese army for three days and nights, and had no alternative but to fight against the Japanese invaders with bayonets. He hacked seven Japanese invaders to death in succession, was shot by a bullet through the heart and died at just 36, with his blood all over the battlefield.

Wan Li's father, Wan Jinshan

Wan Li went to Shanxi and buried the corpse of his father. After his father died for the country, Wan Li lost an uncle and a brother in battle during the war against Japanese aggression. It is said that his uncle was attacked and eaten alive by Japanese wolf dogs and only a pile of bones was left after his death.

Diligent, thrifty, simple and kind, Wan Li's mother, surnamed Niu, was the daughter of an ordinary farmer of Niujuan village, Dongping county. Because her husband left home for a distant place leaving her to care for young children, all the heavy burden of life fell onto her shoulders. She resolutely supported the family and tried to make ends meet by washing, needlework and making hand-woven fabrics. She had to pick up the ears of wheat left in the field under the sun during the wheat harvest and dig up sweet potatoes left in the field after the autumn harvest.

Wan Li's mother, Niu Huifang

Despite the hard life, his mother still tried every means to support Wan Li to study from primary school through junior middle school. Fortunately, Wan Li was a diligent student keen to make progress. Before primary school, Wan Li studied in an old-style private school for one year during which he was able to recite *The Analects of Confucius* (one of the classic works of the Confucian school) deftly. However, without the explanation of a teacher, he read the book without any understanding of it.

Wan Li received primary education in Shuyuan primary school in Dongping county, a senior primary school built in 1904. After six years of schooling, he emerged with a basic modern cultural education.

Wan Li's innate intelligence gradually manifested itself when he studied at Shuyuan primary school. Fond of learning, he endeavoured to make progress and academic achievement. What merits special mention is that Shuyuan primary school had two tennis courts where Wan Li learnt to play tennis and became keen on sports.

In the early 1930s, Wan Li was admitted to Dongping county middle school which was the only middle school and the highest institution of

Wan Li's alma mater - the former Shandong provincial second normal school, now known as Shandong Qufu normal school, on the eastern campus of Qufu normal university

The classroom block of Qufu normal school where Wan Li once studied

learning in Dongping county, with a course length of three years and diverse curricula.

In the autumn of 1933, Wan Li signed up for examinations for two schools concurrently - Shandong provincial first normal school in Jinan (hereafter referred to as 'Jinan first normal school') and Shandong provincial second normal school in Qufu (hereafter referred to as 'Qufu second normal school'). When he was admitted to Qufu second normal school, he received a letter advising him that he had also been enrolled at Jinan first normal school. In the end, Wan Li chose to study at Qufu second normal school simply because of the low living expenses there and a monthly subsidy of Rmb5 for food offered by the school.

Chapter 2

Stifling the December 9th Student Movement

Shandong provincial second normal school was established in Qufu, the hometown of Confucius, a great thinker and educator, in the 1920s. It was one of the four normal schools in Shandong province and the predecessor of Qufu normal school. Fan Mingshu, the head of the four major educators of Shandong in modern times, was once the principal of Shandong provincial second normal school.

Fan Mingshu was a student of Shandong receiving government-sponsored overseas education. He struck a policeman's bayonet with his bare head and led the students of Jinan normal school to rush into the street during the 'May 4th' cultural movement. Advocating an inclusive

Landmark sculpture of Qufu with the inscription: *Confucius's travels to various states in the Eastern Zhou Dynasty*

schooling policy, he was a forerunner promoting enlightenment and progressive education. When he studied in the Qufu second normal school, he supported the patriotic campaigns of the students and bought books and magazines such as *The Communist Manifesto, Das Kapital* and *Guide* written in foreign languages. An atmosphere of researching Marxism-Leninism and discussing the problems in Chinese society developed in the school.

As early as during the May 4th movement, the students of Qufu second normal school launched anti-feudal student campaigns for democracy and forced the stubborn principal to resign.

Wan Li's alma mater - Shandong normal school in Qufu in the 1930s

In the spring of 1926, the Communist Party of China (CPC) second normal school branch was set up and started to organize CPC members' activities around Qufu. Led and influenced by the CPC, the progressive students of Qufu second normal school incessantly launched student movements, witnessing one climax after another. The school gained resounding fame as a consequence and shared the reputation of being the 'communist second normal school' together with Baoding second normal school in the southern and northern parts of China respectively.

In October 1929, progressive teachers and students rehearsed a historic feudal play giving rise to the 'Confucius Meeting Nanzi case' (Nanzi being the wife of Duke Ling of Wei in the Spring and Autumn period), causing a sensation nationwide. The drama satirising Confucius in front of the Kong family mansion caused a stir in Qufu. Just at that time, Inukai Tsuyoshi, a former prime minister of Japan, went to Qufu in the company of national government officials and encountered opposition and taunts during his speech from the students of Qufu second normal school who were afterwards punished severely under the order of Chiang Kai-shek.

Shandong authorities arrested many Qufu second normal school teachers and students in May 1932. The CPC Qufu special branch in Qufu second normal school was practically wiped out, the progressive forces were

Wan Li's desk when he studied at Qufu second normal school

severely damaged but luckily the underground flame of revolution still quietly burnt.

In 1933, Wan Li studied in class 3, grade 8 of Qufu second normal school. Influenced by the revolutionary tradition of the second normal school, he and other progressive students organised a 'study group' in a bid to study progressive books and magazines as well as Marxist works. Filled with admiration for the CPC and the red army and yearning to join the revolutionary base, they rapidly grew to become revolutionary youths. He often mailed copies of *National Salvation Daily* to Wan Danru, his aunt teaching in his hometown and the latter quietly put the newspapers in the chalk holders of other teachers.

Led by the CPC, Beijing students held a large-scale anti-Japanese demonstration on 9 December 1935 which won the support of students in Jinan. Yin Guizhang (Lin Hao), a student and CPC member of the provincial middle school, wrote to Li Jian, a student of Qufu second normal school to notify him of the situation of the 'December 9th' student movement in Beijing in the hope of gaining support from the second normal school students. Li Jian promptly consulted with progressive classmates including Wan Li and Ding Hongze and decided to call on the students of Qufu second normal school to boycott classes and launch street demonstrations.

They held a general students' meeting the next day, notified the students of the situation regarding the patriotic student movements in Beijing and Jinan, and declared a general boycott of classes and street demonstrations after breakfast. However, when the meeting came to an end, the principal of Qufu second normal school abruptly announced the order of the provincial education department that all schools of middle-school level and above should give students a holiday in advance and policemen immediately compelled the students to leave the campus. All these negative efforts nipped the patriotic student movement in the bud.

The auditorium of Shandong provincial normal school in Qufu, where Wan Li, Li Jian and Ding Hongze held a general meeting of students in December 1935 to circulate information about the situation of the patriotic student movements in Beijing and Jinan

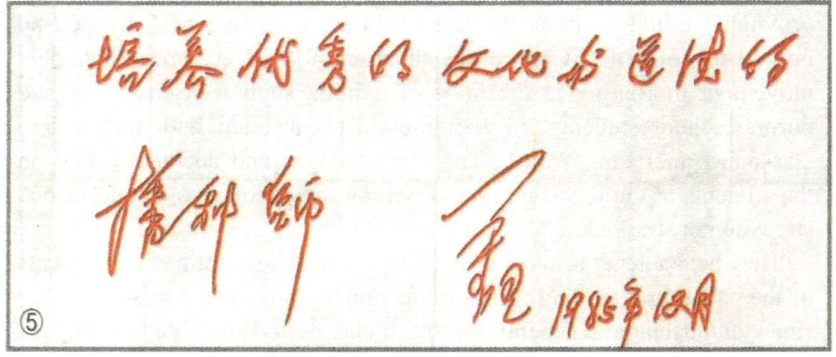

Inscription by Wan Li for Qufu normal school: *Sowing the seeds of fine culture and morality*

In November 1985, Wan Li returns to his alma mater after many years' absence in the company of local provincial and municipal leaders

Chapter 3

Establishing the CPC Dongping County Work Committee in His Home

In early 1936, Dong Linyi, inspector of the CPC western Shandong committee, returned to Dongping county to develop the party organisation. When Dong Linyi went to conduct activities in the rural service training station of the students in Jining normal school in May, he met Wan Li, a student of Qufu second normal school, being trained there and recruited him as a CPC member.

In July 1936, Wan Li graduated from Qufu second normal school, returned to Dongping as dispatched by Dong Linyi and was employed to

Site of the former service training station of the eight provincial normal schools of Shandong in Nanjia village, eastern suburbs, Jining, Shandong. On 1 May 1936, Wan Li was recruited as a CPC member introduced by Dong Linyi

Soon after Wan Li was admitted into the CPC in 1936, he returned to his hometown in Dongping county, Shandong province and taught in Tiandadian Wanquan primary school where he worked for the party and secretly recruited CPC members. At that time, about half of the cadres at county, district and town level came from Tiandadian Wanquan primary school, hence its reputation for being 'half of Tiandadian county'. The picture shows the class bell used by Tiandadian Wanquan primary school since the 1930s

teach in Tiandadian Wanquan primary school in the seventh district. Under the cover of teaching, Wan Li worked secretly for the CPC. Backed up by Principal Tian Zizhen, Wan Li made contact with progressive teachers and students, set up a 'study group', organised others to read the works of such progressive writers as Lu Xun and Zou Taofen, sang progressive operas and made wall posters to publicise the significance of the red army's Long March and the advocacy of the CPC to fight against Japanese aggression and save the nation.

Wan Li introduced Tian Zizhen to be recruited as a CPC member in January 1937 and Zhang Shaoyu, Zhan Yuzhang, Gao Mingxu (Gao Siliang), Wang Ruifu, Xia Huanwu, Xie Yifeng and Liu Canjun as CPC members in March and April. In addition to Wan Li and Tian Zizhen, there were nine other teachers working in the school. Eight of the teachers threw themselves into revolutionary work, which indicated the influence of Wan Li's work.

In the spring of 1937, Wan Li secretly contacted more than 30 progressive teachers in Dongping and set up the Dongping county primary school teachers' joint committee in Shuyuan primary school with Wan Danru, Wan Li's aunt, as president.

During that period, Wan Li often returned to the schools in Dongping county town for clandestine activities and developed progressive teachers to build anti-Japanese organisations. In July, Wan Li introduced Yu Linfu and Meng Ziming to join the party. He and Yu Linfu, director of teaching at Magongci primary school often secretly contacted progressive teachers and students of schools in the county town, held meetings for progressive teachers, students and patriotic figures in Magongci primary school to publicise the CPC's advocacy for fighting against Japanese invaders and saving the nation, held party member conferences and discussed such questions as developing the party organisation and building an anti-Japanese armed force. By then, the party members working for the party in Dongping amounted to 24, including 10 recruited personally by Wan Li. It was imperative to establish the local CPC organisation in Dongping county.

Wan Danru, president of Dongping county primary school teachers' joint committee

Establishing the CPC Dongping County Work Committee in His Home

An artist's impression of the Dongping county work committee led by Wan Li (centre)

In October 1937, with the approval of the CPC Shandong provincial committee, the CPC Dongping county work committee was set up directly led by the CPC Shandong provincial committee. The first conference of the county work committee was held in Wan Li's house in Xijuanpeng street, Zhoucheng town, Dongping county, which was the first county-level party organisation in Taixi, with Wan Li as the secretary, Yu Linfu as the commissar in charge of organisation and Meng Ziming as the commissar in charge of publicity for the work committee.

The county work committee determined its tasks: to energetically mobilise the people and publicise various types of anti-Japanese activities; to mobilise the people to offer their strength, money, guns and knowledge, and to join the anti-Japanese war; to actively cultivate cadres as the backbone of the anti-Japanese war; to positively and prudently recruit new CPC members and expand the strength of the party organisation; to

Building to commemorate the birth of the CPC Dongping county work committee

carry out legitimate struggle; and to build an anti-Japanese armed force and mobilise progressive teachers, students and young farmers to launch an armed uprising.

After the Dongping county work committee was established, Wan Li and his associates positively won over prestigious top elites and intellectuals to join the 'Chinese national liberation vanguard corps (vanguard corps)', set up more than 10 'vanguard corps' and recruited more than 100 such corps members in Qingshuitan third district, Weizihe fifth district, Tiandadian seventh district and Shouzhangji eighth district, including 30 in Magongci primary school in October. During the anti-Japanese war an enormous amount of 'vanguard members' joined the party.

To widely unite with all the patriotic figures to jointly fight against the Japanese invaders and expand the anti-Japanese armed forces, the county work committee decided to establish the 'Dongping county anti-Japanese salvation association' in November 1937, requiring party members and progressive elements to take the lead in joining that organisation. Qiang Renpu worked as the president of the association. The association was tasked to recruit party members, unite with patriotic figures and expand the anti-Japanese armed forces. In late 1937, the association boasted more than 150 members and sponsored the *Anti-Japanese Salvation Weekly* expounding the party's advocacy for fighting against Japanese invaders, reporting information from the front line, raising donations and playing a vital publicity role.

In early 1938, in accordance with an agreement between Fan Zhuxian, commissioner of the Kuomintang's (KMT) sixth administrative region in Shandong province in collaboration with the CPC in the anti-Japanese war, the Dongping county government supervisory council of the KMT invited prestigious intellectuals to be council officials. More than 30 people including Wan Li, Qiang Renpu and Tian Zizhen were invited to work there. They conducted publicity everywhere and initiated nationwide anti-Japanese warfare in their legal capacity as supervisors; they publicised the anti-Japanese war in the KMT sub-unit to urge them to join the nationwide fight against the Japanese invaders.

A reconstruction of the scene of the Dongping county work committee established in Wan Li's home

Wan Li: Resolute Reformer and Legislator

In an effort to eliminate the hard life of the poor people and urge the people to hurl themselves into the anti-Japanese war, Wan Li and the county work committee decided to establish the 'farmers' welfare association' in an area with a superior foundation. Tiandadian was 35km away from Dongping county town at the crossroads of five counties, featuring criss-crossing lakes, inconvenient logistics and inaccessible communications. Wan Li and Tian Zizhen primarily initiated more than 80 impoverished farmers to establish the Tiandadian 'farmers' welfare association'. Afterwards, they set up such associations in more than 10 villages around the Weizi river in the fifth district and recruited more than 200 members

The development of such organisations as 'national vanguard corps', 'associations' and 'welfare associations' awakened the people, spread the influence of the party among the people and laid a fine mass base for anti-Japanese armed uprisings.

Niu Huifang, Wan Li's mother, actively supported Wan Li's revolutionary activities. On the left of the picture is the room in which she stood guard for the work committee when it was in session there

Successive CPC county party secretaries of Dongping county (1937-1947)

Wan Li
October 1937 — August 1938

Qiang Renpu
August 1938 — December 1938

Liu Zhongyu
December 1938 — April 1940

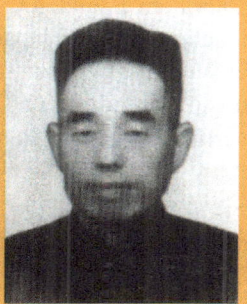

Wang Hecheng
April 1940 — April 1942

Qiang Zizheng
April 1942 — September 1943

Zhao Xiaosan
September 1943 — June 1945

Wang Yuzhen
June 1945 — June 1947

Chapter 4

'Dongping-Wenshang Self-Defense Force' Holds High the Anti-Japanese Banner

After the Marco Polo Bridge Incident, the Japanese army's 10th division advanced southwards into Shandong along the Tianjin-Pukou road. Han Fuqu's KMT troops successively fled in disorder after resistance in northern Shandong. The CPC central committee proposed 10 major guidelines to resist Japanese aggression and save the nation. The northern bureau of the CPC central committee (hereafter referred to as the 'northern bureau') called on 'CPC members to take off the long gown and join the guerrillas'. The Shandong provincial CPC committee formulated 10 major

Early Dongping CPC members

guidelines and plans to launch armed resistance against the Japanese invaders. The anti-Japanese flames burnt in all corners of Shandong. The Dongping county work committee positively publicised the CPC's advocacy for resisting Japan and saving the nation, and the policies of the Chinese united front against Japanese aggression, and mobilised people to join the armed forces against Japan.

The southwestern Shandong CPC work committee was set up in October 1937 with the Dongping county work committee under its leadership. It dispatched CPC member Liu Xing to organise the national salvation movement to resist Japanese aggression in Wenshang county in November 1937. At that time, Wenshang county had no party organisation. Liu Xing consequently came to Dongping county and established contact with Wan Li, then secretary of the county work committee. Wan Li and Liu Xing often discussed the issue of how to build anti-Japanese armed forces and prepare for armed uprising.

In December, Wan Li dispatched Meng Ziming to Jining with his letter and asked the CPC southwestern Shandong work committee for

The people of Dongping-Wenshang initiate a new upsurge of anti-Japanese aggression led by Wan Li

instructions on building the anti-Japanese armed forces. It happened that Japanese aircraft bombed Jining and Meng Ziming lost contact with the CPC southwestern Shandong work committee, returned from Jining to the Weizi river and reported it to Wan Li in Zhao Xiaosan's house. Wan Li wrote to Zhang Jinduo (namely, Zhang Ruogu, one of the people in charge of the Shandong National Salvation Association and then director of the general mobilisation committee of the fifth KMT military zone) and dispatched Meng Ziming and Zhao Xiaosan to Jining to consult with him about the establishment of the anti-Japanese armed forces. En route from Jining to Xuzhou, they finally found Zhang Jinduo and gave him Wan Li's letter.

Zhang Jinduo asked Guo Yingqiu (then the person in charge of the office of the Eighth Route Army in Xuzhou, whose public identity was the director in charge of organisation of the general mobilisation committee of the fifth KMT military zone) to designate the local armed forces in Dongping county as the first column of the second guerrilla headquarters of the fifth military zone in the name of the general mobilisation committee. Guo Yingqiu happened to encounter heavy snow when he returned to Dongping. Jining and other places had been lost and the routes had been cut off. Shanxian county CPC committee secretary Li Yi invited Meng Ziming and others to stay in Shanxian county and launch anti-Japanese activities.

People of Dongping being mobilised to resist the Japanese

'Dongping-Wenshang Self-Defense Force' Holds High the Anti-Japanese Banner

Troops of the eighth branch of the Hebei-Shandong-Henan military zone of the Eighth Route Army with Wan Li as the political commissar and Zeng Siyu as the commander-in-chief hold a conference in Yancunpu town, Fanxian county to celebrate victory in the anti-Japanese war. The picture shows the meeting venue

To find the higher-level party organisation as soon as possible, Wan Li personally came to Liaocheng, found Xu Yunbei who was in charge of the CPC's northwestern Shandong special committee and linked up with the organisation. The county work committee appointed Qiang Renpu as the commissar in charge of publicity and Tian Zizhen as a committee member.

On 5 February 1938, the intellectuals, young students and farmers in Dongping and Wenshang quietly assembled in Yongan temple in Wenshang county by twos and threes under the guise of visiting relatives. Tian Zizhen took three rifles and one handgun, donated 200 silver dollars, led more than 20 people, headed for Yongan temple in Wenshang county, launched an anti-Japanese armed uprising together with more than 100 people mobilised by Liu Xing and Chen Boheng in Wenshang, and set up the 'Dongping-Wenshang People's Anti-Japanese Self-Defense Force'.

The armed force immediately hurled itself into the anti-Japanese war. To cooperate with the Xuzhou battle and contain the enemy, the force made a detour from Yangdian to Baita village in the east of the town, braved a heavy snowfall during the night and destroyed the highway and bridges from Yanzhou to Wenshang. After being discovered by the Japanese army, they waged a fierce combat. Due to their lack of experience in their first fight, some members were dispersed.

Wan Li and Dongping county work committee dispatched CPC members Wang Bomou and Tian Huaixian to gather the scattered soldiers who had returned home in the seventh and eighth districts of Dongping, reorganise them and send them back to the army. On the pretext that anti-Japanese activities should not go across the border, the KMT county government detained Wang Bomou and Tian Huaixian. Wan Li and the county work committee promptly organised their rescue and mobilised the 'vanguard corps' members to hold a meeting in the town to lodge vehement protest against the KMT government, demanding that it release the anti-Japanese activists as soon as possible. Patriotic figures Yang Jingzhai, Guo Fuxian, Dai Fengzhou and Sun Yacheng also carried on negotiations and forced County Magistrate Yao Mengyuan to release Wang Bomou and Tian Huaixian.

Chapter 5

Appointed Director of the CPC's Taixi Special Committee Publicity Department

In May 1938, the CPC central committee appointed Comrade Guo Hongtao as the CPC Shandong provincial committee secretary. When he headed a group of cadres from Yan'an to Shandong by way of Dongping, he listened to Wan Li's report on the work of the county work committee and fully affirmed the committee's work. In June 1938, Comrade Guo Hongtao went eastwards to Beichou village, Feicheng county and established the CPC Taixi special committee with Duan Junyi as the secretary and Wan Li as the publicity department director.

CPC Taixi special committee secretary Duan Junyi

As instructed by Guo Hongtao, Wan Li energetically built up the party, publicised it and organised people. He primarily set up underground liaison stations in Dongping and Jinkou and then incorporated the Huxi anti-Japanese guerrillas. By the end of 1938, the number of CPC members in Taixi had risen from less than 100 to more than 400. In addition, four county or work committees in Tai'an (the western part), Feicheng, Changqing and eastern Wenshang, and anti-Japanese mobilisation committees had been established in all counties on the basis of the Dongping county work committee.

According to the assignment of the special committee, Wan Li came to the Western Shandong People's anti-Japanese Self-Defense Force to consolidate the party organisation and build the army. After training and consolidation, the troops strengthened the party's leadership, implemented strict discipline, eliminated bad elements among the troops and took on a new look. In September 1938, Wan Li and He Guangyu led the anti-Japanese armed forces set up during the uprising in Yongan temple to head for Dongping and mobilised the people. The forces gradually expanded and when the troops conducted activities in Dongping county, they were incorporated into the advance echelon of the 10th detachment together with other anti-Japanese armed forces established by Dongping county work committee and the number of members totalled more than 1,000.

In late 1938, the Western Shandong People's Anti-Japanese Self-Defense Force and the advance echelons were reorganised into the sixth detachment of the Shandong column of the Eighth Route Army in the Dafeng mountainous area of Changqing county, amounting to several

The CPC Taixi special committee that Wan Li served assisted the 115th division in establishing the Taixi anti-Japanese base. The picture shows the conference for the cadres above the battalion level in Changzhuang, Dongping county

Appointed Director of the CPC's Taixi Special Committee Publicity Department

A group photo of senior officers of the 115th division of the Eighth Route Army and local party committee members including Wan Li

thousand, publicly held up the banner of the Eighth Route Army led by the CPC and founded the Taixi anti-Japanese guerrilla base.

After the sixth detachment was set up, the CPC Taixi special committee decided that the troops should head for the mountainous areas of southern Pingyin county, eastern Dong'e county and western Dongping county to establish the Ping'e anti-Japanese base. Wan Li came to Ping'e mountainous area together with the troops. With the efforts of Wan Li and others, the CPC Ping'e county committee was officially set up, which significantly promoted the development of the party organisation and the anti-Japanese armed forces.

Over a period of 10 months, the CPC Taixi special committee established an anti-Japanese base of some scale in the mountainous area to the west of Mount Tai and erected a banner of resistance against Japanese aggression behind the enemy lines.

In March 1939, after the eastward advance detachment of the 115th division of the Eighth Route Army came to Dongping county, the CPC western Shandong committee followed the instructions of the northern bureau and rendezvoused with the Tianjin-Pukou detachment of the Eighth Route Army in Taixi. According to the suggestion of Comrade Luo Ronghuan, the CPC western Shandong committee and the CPC Taixi prefectural committee (formerly called the Taixi special committee) held a conference of activists in the local area and the army in Changzhuang, Dongping county on 20 March 1939. Wan Li made specific preparations for the conference. At the conference, Comrade Luo Ronghuan conveyed the essence of the sixth plenary session of the CPC sixth central committee, analysed the situation in Taixi, affirmed the work of the party organisation and the army of Taixi, and proposed the tasks of immediately building the anti-Japanese democratic regime and constructing the anti-Japanese base.

The conference deeply impressed Wan Li who directly listened to and conveyed the essence of the plenary session of the CPC central committee in his capacity as one of the leaders of the local party committee for the first time. The conference addressed the new situation of the war of resistance against Japanese aggression in Taixi. After the Changzhuang conference, the CPC Taixi prefectural committee, as supported and instructed by the eastward advance detachment, vigorously carried out the work of building the base focusing on party and government building, mass work and the united front.

Wan Li led the work group to do their work in Ping'e mountainous area. The eastward advance detachment and the CPC Taixi prefectural committee highly valued and positively managed the work of the united front, held a Taixi military and political joint conference in Sunbo village, united with a large group of local patriotic dignitaries and fostered a sound and unified situation of resistance against Japanese aggression. Wan Li and the work group also offered instructions to establish anti-Japanese democratic governments in the counties of Dongping and Pingyin.

Luo Ronghuan, successively commander and concurrently political commissar of Shandong military region and political commissar and acting commander of the 115th division during the anti-Japanese war

Appointed Director of the CPC's Taixi Special Committee Publicity Department

Changzhuang in Dongping county - the former site of the headquarters of the 115th division of the Eighth Route Army in the Taixi anti-Japanese base

The former headquarters of the 115th division in Changzhuang, Dongping county

Chapter 6

Lufang Breakout Battle Shocks the Nation

In establishing the Taixi anti-Japanese base, Wan Li and the comrades of the prefectural committee experienced the Lufang breakout combat which shocked the nation. It was another famous combat against the Japanese army launched by the 115th division after the victory at Pingxingguan since the outbreak of the war of resistance against Japanese aggression.

After entering Taixi in early March 1939, the eastward advancing detachment cooperated with the sixth detachment in more than 10 combats, defeated the Japanese army and the puppet army on both banks of the Wenhe river and killed more than 1,000 of the enemy. The Japanese army was shocked by the actions of the detachments and other anti-Japanese efforts in Taixi on a grand and spectacular scale.

In early May, Suetaka Kamezo, the commander-in-chief of the 12th Japanese army stationed in Shandong, mustered Japanese army and puppet army troops totaling more than 8,000 in 17 cities and towns, including Jinan, Tai'an, Feicheng and Yanzhou, and besieged the Taixi anti-Japanese base from nine directions in an attempt to trap all the eastward advancing detachments and the local party, political and military anti-Japanese forces in an action.

At dawn on 11 May, the 115th division headquarters, the CPC western Shandong committee and the Taixi prefectural committee organs, the 686th regiment (excluding the third battalion), the Tianjin-Pukou detachment and the sixth detachment totaling more than 3,000 were besieged in a narrow basin around Lufang, Feicheng county. At that time, the Taixi prefectural committee organs and the 115th division headquarters organised joint activities, and Wan Li and most comrades in the organs were surrounded. Under covering gunfire, the enemy attacked the Chinese army. Chen

Wan Li during the war of resistance against Japanese aggression

Guang, the deputy divisional commander, ordered the 686th regiment to seize the commanding heights, namely, Fat Pig mountain and Yashan mountain, the special forces battalion to seize Dongshan mountain and the Tianjin-Pukou detachment to seize Mount Phoenix in a concerted effort to counterattack the enemy.

This was the first time that Wan Li had experienced such fierce fighting with the sounds of gunshots reverberating around the mountain tops, shouts ringing in his ears, bullets ripping through the air around Lufang and the earsplitting sounds of explosives. The 686th regiment beat back nine successive enemy attacks and the special forces battalion and the Tianjin-Pukou detachment also dealt heavy blows to the enemy. The combat lasted from morning until the afternoon. The enemy made an all-out assault against the 115th division headquarters, with bullets flying in all directions. After relentless counterattacks, our army finally beat back the enemy.

Chen Guang, deputy commander of the 115th division

At 3 or 4 o'clock in the afternoon, the comrades of the Taixi prefectural committee had a simple meal of sweet potatoes and water. The combat continued fiercely and the division headquarters decided to stick it out until nightfall and break out of the encirclement in the night. Wan Li and the comrades of the prefectural committee organs put their knapsacks in the big cellars in the village and planned to advance with light packs. After it got dark, they began to break out of the encirclement along the paths in different directions. Wan Li, together with a comrade and a correspondent of the 115th division, groped his way and tried to rush out on a dark night along a path filled with jagged rocks of grotesque shapes at the red pass. Hungry and thirsty with only some sweet potatoes and some water for one day and one

Lufang Breakout Battle Shocks the Nation

Fierce Lufang breakout combat

night, they felt exhausted. Gritting their teeth, they marched non-stop for 4 to 5km and arrived at the rendez-vous point in Wuyan village, Dongping county the next day.

A few days later, the 115th division held a meeting to celebrate victory in the battle of Lufang; the Taixi prefectural committee organised the cadres and ordinary people to clear up the battlefield and protect and take care of the wounded; the CPC Dongping and Feicheng county committees organised a visit to the troops with a lot of goods and materials.

In the battle of Lufang, the 115th division killed and injured more than 1,300 Japanese soldiers and puppet soldiers, including more than 50 Japanese army officers including a Japanese colonel, with more than 200 casualties. More Japanese soldiers were killed by the Eighth Route Army in this battle than in any other military action in Shandong during the anti-Japanese war. Moreover, it foiled the Japanese army plot to annihilate the 115th division headquarters, the main forces of the division, and the party and government organs in western Shandong and Taixi, and vigorously safeguarded the Taixi anti-Japanese base. The impact of the battle of Lufang astonished the whole nation. Chiang Kai-shek sent a telegram to Zhu De and Peng Dehuai telling them he was 'absolutely delighted' about the battle. This actually acknowledged the legal position of the 115th division in the anti-Japanese war in Shandong.

Wuyan village, Feicheng county where the conference was held by the 115th division to celebrate victory at the battle of Lufang

The former office of Luo Ronghuan in Wuyan village; now a county-level cultural relics protected site

In late August after the breakout combat in Lufang, the western Shandong military and political committee held a conference in Xiao'anshan town, Dongping county to discuss the establishment of the western Shandong plain anti-Japanese base. Luo Ronghuan explained the necessity and possibility of establishing that base at the conference. The conference concluded by agreeing to build such a base. Wan Li was appointed as the deputy secretary of the CPC Yunxi (western Shandong) prefectural committee in late 1939 and as its secretary in November 1940.

Japanese army weapons and ammunition captured at the battle of Lufang

Chapter 7

Landlady Protects Births of Revolutionaries' Descendants

Wan Li and Bian Tao got married in 1940 as a couple in conjugal love after the ordeals of war.

Bian Tao was born to a family in Taiping street, western Changqing county, Shandong in 1920. Her father was a farmer living a life below the average with a small plot of poor land. Living only 30km away from Jinan, her father was imbued with modern thinking and persisted in sending his daughter Bian Tao to study in the county's second primary school despite the fact that he was not very well off.

Wan Li and Bian Tao

Landlady Protects Births of Revolutionaries' Descendants

In the spring of 1932, Bian Tao graduated from primary school and was admitted to the county middle normal school. She made her decision to study there because of her poor family and luckily the county middle normal school did not charge any fees but allocated Rmb2 each month to cover the cost of living during study. Four years later, in the spring of 1936, Bian Tao returned to teach in the Changqing county second primary school which was also her alma mater.

Bian Tao studied seriously and assiduously and read a vast number of progressive books in her spare time. When she served as a teacher, she actively participated in social activities such as fundraising for the victims of natural disasters. She also joined the 'Alma Mater Student Association' of the county middle school to publicise the CPC's advocacy of resisting Japanese aggression. After the anti-Japanese war broke out, Bian Tao committed herself to the struggle to resist Japan and save the nation. In late 1937, Bian Tao joined the CPC-led anti-Japanese armed forces in her hometown. A year and a half later, the CPC Changqing committee recalled her to work in the local rural area and mobilise the women there to join the anti-Japanese war.

After getting married to Wan Li, Bian Tao worked in Yunxi. Amidst the flames of war and the abominable environment, she and Wan Li could not live together but were busy with their own workloads. She lived in a wealthy and influential family in Guduisi village, Danian town, Yuncheng county. She got pregnant for the first time

Bian Tao, Wan Li's wife, and their four children in Heze, Shandong in April 1949

in 1943. She felt extremely worried and did not know where to give birth. It was the prevailing social custom in the local area that the women of other families giving birth in their own family would bring bad luck and disaster.

When she felt perplexed, her landlady candidly told Bian Tao 'not to be awkward and give birth in my house'. As a matter of fact, the landlady was originally the wife of a landlord and was maltreated by her husband because she had not given birth to a boy for him. The landlord married another wife and tortured and beat her mercilessly. She could not bear the humiliation, broke up the family and lived apart with her daughter as a result.

Named Li Manqing, her daughter eyed the dark life of the feudal family since her childhood and was filled with the consciousness of resistance. When Bian Tao mobilised women to participate in the anti-Japanese war, Li Manqing, at only 16 or 17, immediately hurled herself into the cause. With her daughter joining the war, the landlady was also liberated. She was extremely grateful to the CPC and supported the work of Bian Tao and her own daughter devotedly.

A photo taken in the Shandong base in the late 1940s. First from left: Zhu Hui, Zhang Chengxian's wife; third from left: Wan Bo'ao, Wan Li's eldest son; fifth from left: Wan Zhongxiang, Wan Li's second son; sixth from left: Bian Tao, Wan Li's wife; first from right: Wan Jifei, Wan Li's third son

Landlady Protects Births of Revolutionaries' Descendants

Another pregnant woman named Li Hong also lived in her house, who was the wife of Bai Hua, the publicity department director of the CPC Yunxi prefectural committee and later deputy director of Tianjin people's congress. Bian Tao and Li Hong lived in the eastern and western rooms respectively. Guduisi village was often harassed by some enemies. For fear that accidents might happen, Li Manqing's mother dug a tunnel under her bed in the room to a place on the outskirts of the village. Bian Tao and Li Hong tried to persuade her not to dig it for fear that the house would collapse when it rained. Li Manqing's mother said, "It doesn't matter. It is more important to save a life."

The descendants of the two revolutionaries were safely born in the house in succession. It would have been suspicious if babies were to cry loudly in a household of only a mother and a daughter. Li Manqing's mother contacted Wang Meiying in the nearby Yinlou village and asked her to bring up Bian Tao's baby. Wang Meiying was a CPC member and the director of the village women's association for national salvation, and had lost her newborn daughter. It would serve as cover and avoid any attention and suspicion to have her raise the baby. Managing to bear the pain of separation from her child, she hurled herself into the tense anti-Japanese war.

Chapter 8

Continuously Implementing a Bold Delegative Leadership Style

In the spring of 1941, the Japanese army began to launch the 'public security strengthening campaign', 'iron wall encirclement' and 'mopping-up' operations and the situation became tense in the Hebei-Shandong-Henan and western Shandong anti-Japanese base areas. From 1941 to 1942, the Hebei-Shandong-Henan border region suffered from severe drought, plagues of locusts and crop failures in the countryside causing serious economic difficulties. Between enemy pressure and natural disasters, the bases encountered unprecedented hardship and relentlessly shrank in size. There were only six intact counties in the entire north China anti-Japanese base in 1941 and only seven in 1942 including three intact counties in Yunxi led by Wan Li.

To turn around the dire situation and improve their ability to persist in waging protracted guerrilla warfare, in July 1941, the Hebei-Shandong-Henan area and the western Shandong area were incorporated into the Hebei-Shandong-Henan border region and the Yunxi prefectural committee was transformed into the second prefectural committee with Wan Li as the secretary. After that, Wan Li was appointed as the deputy secretary and later secretary of the eighth prefectural committee.

The second prefectural committee led by Wan Li was in the centre of the base. Because the central area in Puyang, Fanxian county and Guancheng county had never been permanently occupied by the Japanese army, it became the steel fortress of the fight against the Japanese puppet army. 'The steel fortress of Puyang, Fanxian county and Guancheng county comprised a mini Yan'an in the border region.' The leaders at every level all highly valued base construction in the harsh environment. In the autumn of 1942, the CPC Hebei-Shandong-Henan regional committee decided to take the campaigns for democracy and people's livelihood and the deep mobilisation of the people as the central tasks of the border region, designate Puyang and Fanxian county as pilot units and promote their experience throughout the region.

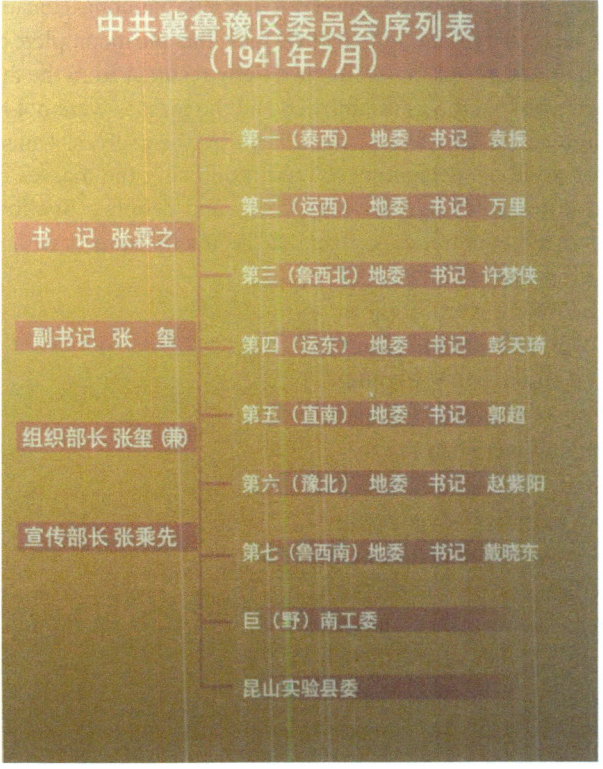

Organisation chart of the CPC Hebei-Shandong-Henan regional committee (July 1941): secretary - Zhang Linzhi; deputy secretary - Zhang Xi; organisation department director - Zhang Xi (concurrent); publicity department director - Zhang Chengxian; first (Taixi) CPC prefectural committee secretary - Yuan Zhen; second (Yunxi) CPC prefectural committee secretary - Wan Li; third (northwest Shandong) CPC prefectural committee secretary - Xu Mengxia; fourth (Yundong) CPC prefectural committee secretary - Peng Tianqi; fifth (Zhinan) CPC prefectural committee secretary Guo Chao; sixth (north Henan) CPC prefectural committee secretary Zhao Ziyang; seventh (southwest Shandong) CPC prefectural committee secretary Dai Xiaodong; South Ju(ye) working committee; Kunshan experimental zone county committee

In the spring of 1944, Duan Junyi and Wan Li sensed the negative mood among farmers in practical work which held back production and was harmful for base construction. Wan Li went to investigate in the rural area to find answers to the problems. At a mass work symposium of the second prefectural committee, the CPC Hebei-Shandong-Henan regional committee secretary Huang Jing held the view that the incomplete campaign for democracy and people's livelihood chiefly resulted from the fact that no correct mass viewpoint was established and the masses were not mobilised because the leaders handled all the affairs by themselves. Consequently, a leadership style of 'delegating to' and mobilising the masses needed to be applied to the campaign for democracy and people's livelihood. Wan Li addressed the conference saying that he totally agreed with Comrade Huang Jing's point of view.

In the following work of up to one year, Wan Li tried to change the work method from running the whole show to delegating and helping the impoverished farmers solve their difficulties and make the most of their own advantages; accurately grasped the policies of the middle farmers; mobilised the masses near the areas occupied by the enemy; developed the work style of seeking truth from facts and summarised the successful experience of the above efforts.

On 27 December 1944, Wan Li delivered a speech *Continuously Implementing a Bold Delegative Leadership Style* at the first district and county cadre conference of the eighth prefectural committee. The speech primarily criticised erroneous practices conducted

Wan Li was a leader who was good at promptly summarising practical work experience

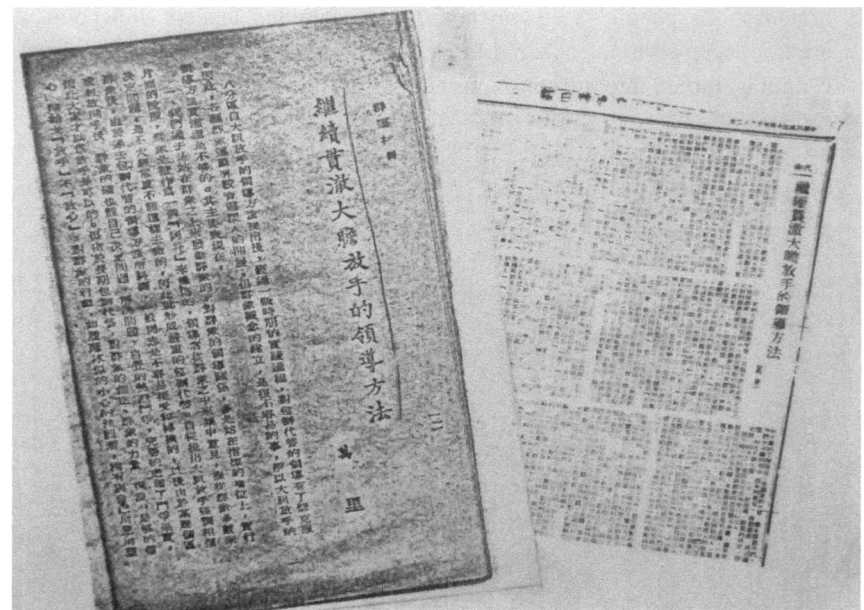

Wan Li's speech at the district and county level conference on 27 December 1944
among the people during base construction. He said: "Some cadres still place themselves above the people when mobilising them, try to control and manipulate people like 'puppets' and attach little priority to soliciting people's views and delegating the majority of decision-making to the people, creating a serious case of doing everything themselves to the exclusion of others."

"Some cadres are not sufficiently confident in the creativity and power of the people. They 'delegate' without 'resting assured', micromanage, try to 'persuade' and 'enlighten' people who disagree with them and bring them round to their point of view. The so-called 'persuasion' and 'enlightenment' are simply superficial 'persuasion' but essentially they demand people's 'obedience'. If people do not obey, cadres handle everything by themselves."

Wan Li also introduced some experiences of the second prefectural committee in the campaign for democracy and people's livelihood and especially stressed the importance of establishing bottom-up people's organisations. Wan Li said: "Without establishing bottom-up people's organisations, people's views are not properly solicited, leaders' viewpoints are not accepted by or adhered to by the people, and the party's policies cannot be turned into the conscious actions of the people."

Wan Li's working paper *Several Harmful Trends in In-depth Work and How To Overcome Them* published in *The Lighthouse* in 1941

Wan Li's article *Giving Scope to the People's Enthusiasm and Creativity* was published on the first page of the *Hebei-Shandong-Henan Daily* on 30 January 1947

Continuously Implementing a Bold Delegative Leadership Style

Deng Xiaoping and Wan Li in front of the pine greeting guests on Huangshan mountain, Anhui province in the summer of 1979

The speech discussed leadership style. It would be the essence of the campaign for democracy and people's livelihood and the key to achieving base construction that genuinely respected the people, solicited their views and transformed the leaders' views into the people's views.

Wan Li's article *Continuously Implementing a Bold Delegative Leadership Style* was reprinted in the *Hebei-Shandong-Henan Daily* on 20 May 1945 as a 'reference text' to direct the campaign for democracy and people's livelihood in the Hebei-Shandong-Henan border region. The article was fully affirmed by Deng Xiaoping who was going all out to research such campaigns.

At the mass work conference of the CPC Hebei-Shandong-Henan branch on 6 June 1945, the campaign for democracy and people's livelihood in the Hebei-Shandong-Henan border region was profoundly analysed. Wan Li attended the conference and listened to Deng Xiaoping's report. It was the first time Wan Li met Deng Xiaoping.

Chapter 9

Total Support for the Liu-Deng Army

The Chinese civil war (between the CPC and the KMT) broke out all over on 26 June 1946. The first round of attacks and counterattacks were most critical and powerful. From 10 August to 31 October 1946, the army of Liu Bocheng and Deng Xiaoping (hereafter referred to as the 'Liu-Deng army') successively triumphed in the battles of Longhailu, Dingtao, Juye and Zhennan and annihilated more than 30,000 enemy troops in total. The battle of Dingtao was praised by Chairman Mao Zedong 'to have been a turning point in the war situation'.

The soldiers and civilians of the seventh prefectural committee of the CPC Hebei-Shandong-Henan committee under Secretary Wan Li went all-out to support the frontline. The picture shows women hurrying to make lined clothes for the People's Liberation Army (PLA) officers and fighters

The four battles of the Liu-Deng army received all-out support from the Hebei-Shandong-Henan liberated area. The battles in Juye and Zhennan were waged in the region of the second prefectural committee. Wan Li organised the whole region to shoulder the onerous task of supporting the front line.

In total, 3,350,500 work points (a method of calculating payment for labour) of the civilian workers - including 8,000 from Juye county, Juancheng county and Yuncheng county and 10,000 from Kunshan county - were applied in the Juye battle. Jiaxiang county sent more than 300 stretchers to the frontline. When the battle came to an end, Wan Li immediately held the CPC county committee secretary joint conference which decided to establish the civilian war service headquarters of the second district as the prevailing independent institution directly under the leadership of the prefectural committee.

In the southern Juancheng battle, the Liu-Deng army adopted the military strategy of a surprise attack which imposed heavy tasks and huge pressure on Wan Li's combat service headquarters to offer prompt support. Wan Li urgently mobilised everyone in the area and applied more than 1.4 million work points to guarantee the progress of the battle.

Civilian workers and militia taking grain to support the front line

People energetically supporting the front line in the southwestern Shandong battle

In November 1946, the Hebei-Shandong-Henan region went through zoning regulations once again and Wan Li worked as the seventh special prefectural committee secretary and political commissar of the military subdistrict. He delegated to and mobilised the people, stimulated an upsurge in land reform, persisted in guerrilla warfare, strengthened the construction of the military subdistrict, the county production brigade, the district squadron and the armed work team, participated in 152 combats big and small, and liberated two counties from March to April 1947. By May, the seventh special prefecture had changed from a guerrilla area to a liberated area under the control of the CPC.

In the early summer of 1947, Wan Li was promoted to CPC Hebei-Shandong-Henan committee secretary and joined hands with Zhang Xi, Zhao Jianmin and Xu Chengbei to lead the work south of the Yellow river. His first act after taking office was to help the Liu-Deng army fight its way across the Yellow river into southwestern Shandong and wage the southwestern Shandong battle.

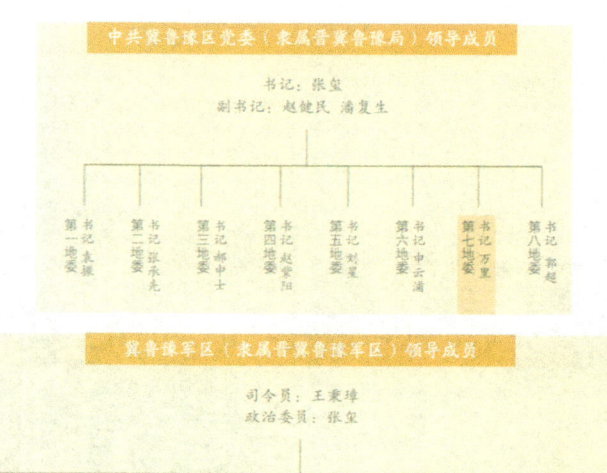

The organization charts above show (top chart) leaders of the CPC Hebei-Shandong-Henan committee (affiliated to the Shanxi-Hebei-Shandong-Henan bureau): secretary - Zhang Xi; deputy secretaries - Zhao Jianmin, Pan Fusheng; first CPC prefectural committee secretary - Yuan Zhen; second CPC prefectural committee secretary - Zhang Chengxian; third CPC prefectural committee secretary – Hao Zhongshi; fourth CPC prefectural committee secretary – Zhao Ziyang; fifth CPC prefectural committee secretary – Liu Xing; sixth CPC prefectural committee secretary – Shen Yunpu; seventh CPC prefectural committee secretary – Wan Li; eighth CPC prefectural committee secretary – Guo Chao. The lower chart shows leaders of the Hebei-Shandong-Henan military region (affiliated to the Shanxi-Hebei-Shandong-Henan military region): commander – Wang Bingzhang; political commissar – Zhang Xi; first military subregional commander – Zhou Guisheng; political commissar – Yuan Zhen; second military subregional commander – Zhang Gangjian; political commissar – Zhang Chengxian; third military subregional commander – Guo Yingqiu; political commissar – Hao Zhongshi; fourth military subregional commander – Li Jingyi; political commissar – Zhao Ziyang; fifth military subregional commander – Liu Dehai; political commissar – Liu Xing; sixth military subregional commander – Zhu Ziwei; political commissar – Shen Yunpu; seventh military subregional commander – He Guangxue; political commissar – Wan Li; eighth military subregional commander – Cui Ting; political commissar – Guo Chao

Total Support for the Liu-Deng Army

From 30 June to 27 July 1947, the Liu-Deng army successively participated in the Yuncheng battle, the Dingtao battle, the Dushanji and Liuyingji battles in Juye and the Yangshanji battle in Jinxiang county, annihilated four reorganised divisions totally including nine brigades numbering 56,000 people, disrupted the strategic deployment of the KMT on the southern battlefront, opened up the way to march into the Dabie mountains and paved the way for strategic attacks.

As the southwestern Shandong battle raged fiercely, local leaders including Wan Li organised local troops to cooperate in the fighting and go all out to accomplish the onerous tasks of guaranteeing combat service support. More than 2,300 stretchers were sent from the seventh special prefecture to the three battles in Yuncheng, Jinxiang and Jining.

Women ground flour and made shoes for the launch of counterattacks. The rumbling noise of flour being ground could be heard deep into the night in Dongping, Wenshang, Jiaxiang and Nanwang counties, and women's shadows flickered in the lamplight as they made military shoes at night. In only 20 days, the women of the seventh special prefecture made 200,000 pairs of military shoes, guaranteeing the needs of the Liu-Deng army.

Dongping was liberated in late 1947. The picture shows PLA troops marching into Dongping county. Wan Li then served as the CPC Hebei-Shandong-Henan committee member and secretary

To support the Jinan battle, Dongping county set up a front-line support headquarters to guarantee supplies to the armed forces, contributing to the victory in the Jinan battle. Pictured above is the *Summary of the Work to Support the Front Line in the Battle to Liberate Jinan* written by the Dongping county front-line support headquarters in October 1948

Chapter 10

Taking Control of Nanjing and Governing the Southwest

On 29 October 1948, the CPC's north China bureau decided to integrate cadres from the CPC committees in Hebei, Shandong, Henan and other areas, reorganise the leading group from district committees into district party committees, and to prepare for wholesale readjustment. Wan Li participated in the work to lead cadres in their preparations for their work in the south.

In late 1948, the CPC Hebei-Shandong-Henan committee integrated cadres from party, government and military organs and 80 cadres from the organs directly under the jurisdiction of the district party committee totaling 3,360 from 210 districts, 30 counties and seven regions. In addition,

Before the campaign to cross the Yangtze river in April 1949, Wan Li led 620 cadres and 120 workers to take control of Nanjing. Pictured (above left) is a traffic permit of the Nanjing military control commission. Pictured (right) is a list of leading cadres of the fifth corps of the second field army of the PLA march south: commander - Fu Jiaxuan (chief of staff of the Hebei-Shandong-Henan military region); political commissar – Xu Yunbei (deputy CPC Hebei-Shandong-Henan committee secretary); deputy political commissar – Shen Yunpu (publicity department director of the CPC Hebei-Shandong-Henan committee) and concurrently director of the political department; chief of staff – Wan Li (CPC Hebei-Shandong-Henan committee secretary general)

there were 1,330 miscellaneous workers and correspondents concerned. Therefore, the total number of people involved topped 4,690. From late February to early March 1949, the cadre detachment of the fifth corps of the second field army of the PLA marched southwards with Wan Li as the chief of staff. After the cadres marching southwards were centralised, Wan Li was in charge of their study and training. The whole detachment studied and received military training for a month there.

Wan Li on the bank of the Yangtze river when he served as the military representative in Pukou district, Nanjing after Nanjing was liberated in 1949

The southbound cadre detachment arrived in Hefei on 7 April 1949. The CPC east China bureau decided to designate Wan Li to take control of Nanjing with 540 cadres. On 23 April 1949, the PLA occupied Nanjing and the counter-revolutionary KMT government that had ruled China for 22 years collapsed. Wan Li led the cadres south into Nanjing. He was appointed as deputy director of the accounting and finance committee, director of the economic department and director of the construction bureau of the military control committee, and began to busy himself with the work to take over and rebuild Nanjing.

On 20 October 1949, Liu Bocheng and Deng Xiaoping led the second field army headquarters out of Nanjing to fight in Sichuan and Guizhou to liberate the southwestern part of China according to the strategic deployment of the central committee. Wan Li marched westwards with the army as ordered. On 1 December 1949, the second field army entered Chongqing.

Wan Li, his wife Bian Tao, his daughter Wan Shupeng and his fourth son Wan Jifei when he worked as director of the industrial department of the southwestern military and administrative commission in the early 1950s

Wan Li: Resolute Reformer and Legislator

Wan Li worked as the deputy director and then director of the industrial department of the southwestern military and administrative commission.

Wan Li pictured in front of Tiananmen on a visit to Beijing from Chongqing to attend a meeting in the autumn of 1952

Wan Li, his wife and daughter in their house in Chongqing

During his work as deputy director and then director of the industrial department, Wan Li tried to explore ways to develop industry and highly valued the reform of the personnel and wage systems. At the staff congress of the Dadukou Steelworks on 14 January 1950, Wan Li stressed that one critical point in managing a plant well was to implement personnel system reform. "Engineers and workers are the masters of the factory and the main force of production". "The engineers' technical skills and the workers' labour deserve respect" and "everybody has specific skills, whose talent should not be obscured". Wan Li explained his view on the question of why engineers were paid more than workers, and told workers and engineers that "anyone with higher ability and skills can be paid more and rewarded for their expertise".

Wan Li and several other Chongqing leaders all lived in manor houses in downtown Chongqing. With large gardens and well located, the residences had panoramic views of the mountain city from their large balconies. One day, Wan Li's two sons and daughter were playing on the balcony, saw some cobblestones in the corner of the balcony and played a game of stone throwing.

While they were playing in high spirits, cries came abruptly from downstairs. Outside the wall was a street and the stones thrown by the children had hit a child passing by downstairs on the head. Some passers-by and the child's parents took the bleeding child to Wan Li's house. Sensing an imminent disaster, the three children hurried off to hide somewhere downstairs.

Wan Li happened to be at home that day. He received the common people at his door, apologised to them and immediately had the child whose head had been hit sent to the hospital by car.

Sending the people away, Wan Li returned to scold his children who were hiding silently in their grandma's room. Wan Li burst in and shouted: "How dare you hit people with stones? This is abuse of power and suppression of ordinary people. That is really going too far! You are no different than the KMT!"

Wan Li was stopped by his mother as he shook his fist. She said, "Don't get so angry with the children. They don't know any better. I'll give them a beating if it is unavoidable!"

Pushing Wan Li away, his mother closed the door, beat each child several times and then said sincerely: "You should not behave so improperly. Even the king is subject to the law. You will pay for death with your own life."

The children cried and said: "We did not intend to hit others. We only threw stones competitively for fun rather than intentionally. We will not throw stones anymore."

Wan Li's mother and her two grandsons Wan Bo'ao and Wan Zhongxiang in the early 1950s

In the evening, their grandmother asked them not to cry, gave her second grandson Wan Zhongxiang a piece of sugarcane and asked him to have supper in the dining hall downstairs. Wan Zhongxiang went downstairs and happened to see Wan Li walking towards him. Wan Li, who ordinarily loved his children very much, flew into a rage and kicked the sugarcane to pieces. Wan Zhongxiang looked ashen, turned round and ran away.

This was the only time in his life that the son saw his father get so violently angry. Wan Li and his wife used to be teachers, accustomed to neither cursing nor beating their children. But on that occasion he did get angry with his children.

Chapter 11

Buying White Curtains for His Mother with His Allowances

In 1952, Wan Li was designated to work as the director and Bian Tao as the section chief of the urban construction department in Beijing. At that time, Wan Li's family lived in Dongsi subdistrict while the department was located in Baiwanzhuang. Although the couple worked in the same department, Wan Li handled affairs justly and never allowed his wife to go to work in his car. Every morning, Bian Tao got up, did the housework, took a bus alone and changed buses two or three times to get to work. Only occasionally, when it snowed heavily, was she allowed to go to work in Wan Li's car.

Wan Li and his wife were very respectful of his mother. Even so, Wan Li never sent his sick mother to the hospital in his government car but hired trishaws instead. His mother loved watching plays, but Wan Li and his wife never abused their power by asking for free tickets for her. His mother was fair-minded and always said to them: "Don't send me there. I can go there by myself."

A group photo of Wan Li's family in their house in Dingjiakeng outside Yongdingmen, Beijing in 1970. From left: Wan Li's eldest son Wan Bo'ao, Wan Li, his mother, his third son Wan Jifei, daughter Wan Shupeng, fourth son Wan Xiaowu, wife Bian Tao and second son Wan Zhongxiang

Buying White Curtains for His Mother with His Allowances

Wan Li and his mother at his house in Beijing

The old lady often went to watch plays in the theatre with her bound feet and bought tickets for the seats on the edge to save money. Seeing the old lady act that way, Beijing opera artists such as Zhang Junqiu and Yun Yanming said to Wan Li's eldest son Wan Bo'ao: "We often see a grey-haired old lady watching our plays in the remotest corner. Later on, we knew that she was Wan Li's mother, your grandmother!"

On the afternoon of Friday, 8 January 1954, Wan Li's second son Wan Zhongxiang solemnly swore an oath at a ceremony, wore a bright red scarf and became the first young pioneer of the Wan family. When Zhongxiang returned home on Saturday (he normally lived on campus), Wan Li and Bian Tao felt extremely excited to see their son returning with the red scarf around his neck. They had made it clear beforehand that they would buy a pair of skates for the first young pioneer.

Early on Sunday morning, Wan Li and Bian Tao took their three children to buy the skates in the Dongsi people's market. Wan Zhongxiang gladly selected a pair of Beibingyang-brand skates worth Rmb25. When it was time to pay, Wan Zhongxiang noticed his brother Wan Bo'ao lowering his head silently beside him and looking at the skates in his hands with admiration. Bo'ao was one year older than Zhongxiang, who was one year late for school due to their unsettled life during wartime and studied in the same class as Zhongxiang in Yucai primary school. Seeing the despondent look of his brother, Zhongxiang was embarrassed and promptly said to his parents: "Please buy a pair of skates for my brother to encourage him to be a young pioneer as soon as possible."

Their parents smiled at each other and responded immediately: "Let's buy a pair for Bo'ao!" Then they bought a pair of skates of the same brand for Bo'ao. They spent a total of Rmb50 for the skates. When the children returned to school with the skates on their back and skated quickly on the skating rink, they felt quite happy and proud. Bo'ao made more of an effort and became a young pioneer shortly thereafter.

Wan Li was a cadre at ministerial level and Bian Tao was a department leader. Their monthly salaries were not high. But they had to support a family of eight and subsidise their destitute relatives. They lived frugally; the children wore handed-down clothes with patches on patches; they often failed to make ends meet at the end of a month.

Soon afterwards, the conflicts between Wan Li and his mother shocked the children. Then Wan Li's family lived in a quadrangle dwelling in Yanle lane, Dongcheng district. Wan Li lived in the northern house with two small bedrooms and one living room. The southern house had two rooms, one for Wan Li's mother and one worker's room. The children lived in their dormitories on workdays and lived either in their grandma's room or slept on the living room floor in the northern house after they returned home on Saturday.

One Sunday, their grandma came into the living room and screamed at Wan Li: "Wan Li, am I not a person? Why were curtains installed in your room rather than mine?"

The fact was that the government installed curtains in the northern house Wan Li lived in without installing any curtains in the southern room. Wan Li's mother found out and came to question him about it.

Wan Li responded: "The state is undergoing financial hardship. I didn't ask the government to install curtains in your room for fear that the government would spend more money."

Buying White Curtains for His Mother with His Allowances

Before liberation, Wan Li's mother washed other people's clothes to supplement the household income. Pictured above is the beetling stone frequently used by Wan Li's mother and stored in Wan Li's former house

His mother refuted: "Don't you have allowances? Can't you buy me curtains with your allowances?"

Wan Li had nothing to say in reply but promised repeatedly and hurried to install curtains of only a single layer of white cloth in his mother's room with his own salary as soon as possible.

The children felt ashamed for having asked their parents to buy them skates. How wonderful it would have been to buy curtains for their grandma with that money! It was the first and only time in their lives that they saw their grandma lose her temper with their father and blame him. From then on, the children did not ask their parents to buy them anything.

Chapter 12

Helping Premier Zhou Build the Great Hall of the People

The CPC central committee held an enlarged meeting of the political bureau in Beidaihe in August 1958 at which it decided to build 10 major construction projects in Beijing, including the great hall of 10,000 people, and required them to be completed and put into use before the 10th anniversary of the founding of the PRC in 1959. The Beijing people's government was directly tasked to sponsor these activities.

The 10 major buildings included: the Great Hall of the People (the name of the hall at that time), the Museum of the Chinese Revolution, the Military Museum of the Chinese People's Revolution, the National Art Museum of China, the National Agriculture Exhibition Centre, the Beijing Workers' Sports Complex, the Diaoyutai State Guest House, the Overseas Chinese Hotel, the National Hotel, the Cultural Palace of Nationalities and the Beijing Railway Station. Among them, the Great Hall of the People headed the 10 major projects, and was guided by Premier Zhou Enlai with Wan Li as the general director on site.

As early as 12 May 1956, the State Administration of Urban Construction was changed into the Urban Construction Department with Wan Li as the director. In 1958, Wan Li was appointed as the secretary of the secretariat of the CPC Beijing municipal committee and deputy mayor of Beijing. On 8 September 1958, Wan Li made a report at the 'Beijing national day project mobilisation conference' to more than 1,000 experts in design and construction units in Beijing.

As to the suspicion and condemnation of some international views about the new China, Wan Li said in his report: "Some people do not believe we can build a modernised country but believe we are good for nothing. We must try to make a good showing and respond with our deeds and facts."

In October 1958, Wan Li (fifth from left), deputy general director of the Beijing '10 major buildings' project, reported the design plan for Tiananmen square to the CPC. Mao Zedong, Liu Shaoqi, Zhou Enlai, Li Fuchun and Peng Zhen listened to the report

It was just under 400 days away from the 1959 national day. Other famous buildings in the world in the same period – such as the UN Headquarters in New York - was built in seven years, the Palace of Nations (Palais des Nations) in Geneva was built in eight years and the Sydney Opera House started construction one year later, and took 14 years to build.

Beijing municipal government immediately invited the national architectural circles in the name of the Architectural Society of China. In only three days, more than 30 top-notch architects from 17 provinces and cities gathered in Beijing, including Liang Sicheng, Yang Tingbao, Zhang Kaiji and Wu Liangyong.

Thirty-four design units in Beijing and dozens of building experts in Shanghai, Nanjing, Guangzhou and Liaoning proposed more than 400 designs. After seven rounds of review, summary and modification, finally Premier Zhou Enlai approved them for implementation. The whole process took only 35 days.

Peng Zhen and Liu Ren, the first and second people in charge of the CPC Beijing municipal committee, attended to the designs personally. Secretary Liu Ren walked on site for measurement and finally decided to expand the building site of the Great Hall of the People from 70,000 to 170,000sqm. In the last round of reviews, Premier Zhou asked Wan Li: "What does the Beijing municipality think about this?" Wan Li told him about the design scheme of the Beijing municipal planning bureau.

After the scheme was passed, the 10,000 people auditorium took up half of the building area of the Great Hall of the People. How to free the people from feeling constrained while guaranteeing the absolute safety of the ceiling? The architects could do nothing to solve the problem.

After long contemplation, Premier Zhou quoted the poem of the 'rosy setting sun and lone ducks' to inspire chief designer Zhang Bo. He said: "One does not feel that the sky is very high when one's feet are on the ground nor that the sea is very far when one is beside the sea. The 'rosy setting sun and lone ducks' should inspire us. Why don't we start from the artistic conception that water and sky merge in one colour and make some abstraction?"

Wan Li (first from left) accompanies Zhou Enlai and others to examine the design model of the Great Hall of the People in March 1959

Suddenly enlightened, Zhang Bo designed three rounds of ripple-shaped dark and light troughs in the dome of the hall echoing the light blue plastic hanging blinds, glistening when the lights were on. The architects installed up to 500 lights in the whole dome so that the audience could look up and see 'constellations of stars' in the vast night sky.

When Wan Li made his mobilisation report in September, the construction team had begun to prepare the materials and machinery to be used. When the design scheme was approved on 16 October, the construction team entered the site and began to level the foundation and make earth pre-pressure tests.

'Centralising advantageous military strength, launching key assaults and waging a war of annihilation' became the magic weapon of the project headquarters to organise construction and rapid progress. According to the statistics, in the whole process of construction, totally more than 1,000 combats, big and small, were organised one after another. The big and small combats showed the key points and the whole picture, and made it possible to turn a series of minor victories into major victories.

In July/August 1959, the interior decoration of the 10,000-people auditorium entered the stage of decisive engagement. The only way out

Through expansion in 1959, Tiananmen square became more magnificent and spacious. The Great Hall of the People on the western side of the square heads the '10 major buildings' built in Beijing in the 1950s

The Military Museum of the Chinese People's Revolution is one of the '10 major buildings' built in Beijing in the 1950s

to finish decorating in just over one month was to centralise the military strength for large-formation warfare. Everything went in full swing in the whole 10,000-people auditorium and all types of work were in operation in the right places so as to finish at a stroke. The difficulty remained that it was necessary to erect all-round scaffolding more than 30 metres from the ground to make the suspended ceiling but up to 10,000 seats could not be installed concurrently since the ground was occupied.

Wan Li listened to the views of all sides attentively and directly made friends with the workers including Li Ruihuan who solved the technical problem of enlarged samples and Zhang Baifa overcoming the difficulties with steel crossmembers. Workers proposed to erect a fir pole on the steel roof truss and suspend the scaffolding downwards. Consequently, in the arch space of the 10,000-people auditorium, construction of eight or nine items such as the walls, ceiling, floor, proscenium arch and second balcony was conducted at the same time creating a spectacular scene which was called the 'battle of the arch'.

As organised by Wan Li, the party, political, workers' and league organisations of all levels on the construction site directly combined meticulous ideological work with the objective of accomplishing the national day project and carried out all publicity and educational activities in a bid to continuously promote project construction. At each stage or critical moment of construction, Wan Li would hold meetings for construction managers to summarise the work of the previous stage and to propose requirements for the next stage.

In the small hours of 9 September 1959, Chairman Mao personally visited the construction site of the Great Hall of the People, came to the two-storey balcony of the Great Hall and inspected the layout of the second storey. He sat down on a newly installed seat with great interest to check whether it was proper and whether there was a clear view of the platform from there. He asked: "Is it safe when so many people sit together?" Wan Li promptly responded: "Chairman Mao, absolutely no problem."

Wan Li said the project had not been named and the premier had mentioned it should be named by Chairman Mao. Chairman Mao asked what they called it. Wan Li responded that workers called it the construction site of the Great Hall, and that they were accustomed to calling it the Great Hall of the People's Congress, the Great Hall or the People's Palace. Chairman Mao said: "'Palace' usually reminds people of feudalism." Wan Li added: "Someone suggested it be called 'the Great Hall of the National People's Congress'". After consideration, Chairman Mao regarded it as too long and suggested that it should be called the Great Hall of the People

The Cultural Palace of Nationalities is one of the '10 major buildings' built n Beijing in the 1950s

The next day, Chairman Mao praised Wan Li: "I saw the newly-built Great Hall of the People yesterday which has been built at great-leap-forward speed! The secretary of the CPC Beijing municipal committee is surnamed Wan and his first name is Li. He is not an easy man because he can cover 10,000 li (5,000km) in one day!"

The National Agriculture Exhibition Centre is one of the '10 major buildings' built in Beijing in the 1950s

On 1 October 1962, people from all walks of life celebrated the 13th anniversary of the founding of the PRC. The picture shows Wan Li (second from left), who was secretary of the CPC Beijing municipal committee secretariat and deputy mayor of Beijing, accompanying party and state leaders including Mao Zedong, Liu Shaoqi, Zhou Enlai and Deng Xiaoping on the Tiananmen gate tower

Chapter 13

Sending His Eldest Son Wan Bo'ao for 10 Years' Rural Labour

In the early 1960s, China was just recovering from the three years of natural disasters with its economy in a stage of recovery and the state called for going in for agriculture in a big way. Wan Bo'ao, Wan Li's eldest son, was 18 years old and had just graduated from senior middle school. Wan Li, then secretary of the CPC Beijing municipal committee secretariat and first deputy mayor of Beijing, decided to send him to get practical experience at Huangfan district farm in Henan province, which encountered resistance from the whole family. Wan Li especially held a family meeting, called on all the family members, old and young and gave them ideological work.

In a small quadrangle dwelling in Yanle lane, Dongcheng district, Beijing on an autumn evening in 1962, eight members of Wan Li's family, old and young, were all grey-faced in the solemn atmosphere. Wan Li's 70-year-old mother sobbed now and then.

Wan Li broke the silence. He looked at his son and said: "I'm a CPC member. I love you indeed. People love their children in different ways, spoiling them in the greenhouse or tempering them in

18-year-old Wan Bo'ao on the Huangfan district farm in Henan

the storm. As for me, I've decided to send you to the frontline of agriculture to gain practical experience."

Wan Li added: "You should remold your ideology, take on the tasks as qualified revolutionary successors and carefully study the works of Chairman Mao and *How to Be A Good Communist* by Liu Shaoqi. Only when you combine with the workers and the farmers can you show your promise. The rural area will provide you with a vast space for great achievements. Maxim Gorky did not study at university but he became one of the litterati in the end."

Nobody could change Wan Li's decision. Wan Bo'ao's grandma finally had to shout to Wan Li: "Let him take your leather coat to keep himself warm." Even that request was refused by Wan Li.

Wan Li said smilingly to his mother: "I will not give the leather coat or even a cent to him. You know, I aim to train him to be self-reliant. But he can take with him the food expenses this month." Pondering for a moment, he added: "I will not give him money but I will vigourously support him to buy books and newspapers."

Wan Li solemnly raised a request to Wan Bo'ao: "Keep away from the idea of returning. It won't do if you want to escape. Unless you escape abroad where I cannot reach you, I'll not allow you to come in the house even when you escape and stand at the door."

Pictured left: Letters written by Wan Li to his eldest son Wan Bo'ao when he was labouring on a farm in Henan before the spring festival of 1963
Pictured right: Wan Bo'ao (left) learning grape management skills from veteran horticultural workers on the Huangfan district farm in Henan province

Sending His Eldest Son Wan Bo'ao for 10 Years' Rural Labour

A report entitled: 'The Son of the Municipal Party Committee Secretary Joins Agricultural Production' relating the tale of Wan Li's eldest son Wan Bo'ao working hard, learning modestly and making progress on the Huangfan district farm in Henan carried on the front page of *China Youth Daily* on 24 September 1963

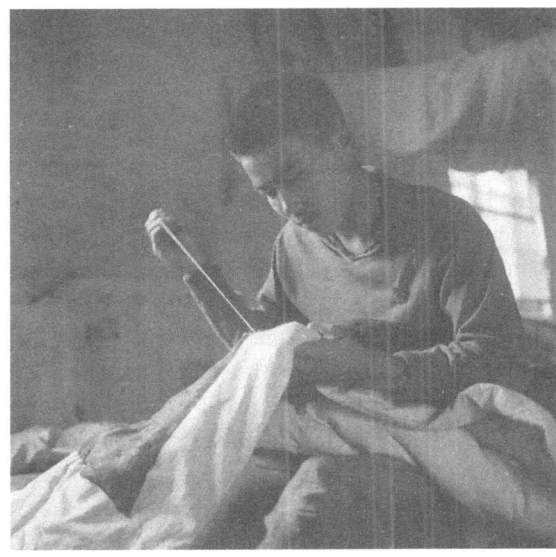

Wan Bo'ao kept the good habit of living frugally and working hard. The picture shows Wan Bo'ao sewing and mending his quilt with cotton wadding

Eldest son Wan Bo'ao engaged in rural labour for 10 years. Keeping his father's instructions firmly in mind, Wan Bo'ao gained practical experience and grew up on the front line of agricultural production

Seeing his father leave no leeway, Wan Bo'ao was absolutely determined: "I'll commit myself fully and resolutely to follow my father's arrangements and show him what I can do!" Before Bo'ao left, Wan Li, who had never written any inscription, wrote down two lines of words on the thick notebook, reading 'stick it out whenever your mind tends to waver'. Wan Bo'ao set out on his journey with the baggage of his parents in times of war, two books and food expenses of Rmb15 for the first month.

Wan Bo'ao became the first child of a cadre in the capital city to support rural construction, which was reported on the front page of the *China Youth Daily* at that time.

After Wan Bo'ao left, his younger brothers and sisters wrote to him and told him their grandma and mother often shed tears; especially, his second younger brother living in the same dorm in the same school with him could not help crying silently when he saw the empty bed in which his brother had once slept; his family members did not know how he was getting along in the remote, tough area.

Wan Li wrote a total of 17 or 18 letters (the most among his five children) to Wan Bo'ao from 1962 through 1966 after his eldest son left for the farm. In the very beginning, Wan Li was worried whether his son's mind would be swayed and if he would escape from the extreme difficulties to everyone's knowledge in those years. But later, he showed more care for the local farmers and inevitably inquired about the production and life of the farmers there in his letters.

Sending His Eldest Son Wan Bo'ao for 10 Years' Rural Labour

Wan Bo'ao picking and carrying fruit in the farm's orchard

Wan Bo'ao labouring and remembering to learn

Wan Bo'ao narrating his father's letters in an interview with Hong Kong's Phoenix TV

With the encouragement of his father, Wan Bo'ao finally stuck it out and worked in the countryside for 10 years. Without any complaint and selflessly devoting himself, he became a model for the nationwide educated youth and was praised by Premier Zhou Enlai. Thanks to his outstanding performance, he was recommended to be a worker-peasant-soldier student and study at university. After graduation from university, he enlisted in the army and became a PLA officer. Years later, he was transferred to work in a certain artillery troop in Beijing and only then did he return to his home after being away for more than 20 years.

Chapter 14

Subjected to Criticism and Struggle with Three Model Workers on New Year's Eve

The fuse that ignited the 'Cultural Revolution' was the article *Comment on the New Edition of the Chronicle Play 'Hai Rui Dismissed from Office'* published in the Shanghai *Wen Hui Bao* in November 1965. In the article, Yao Wenyuan mentioned the name of Wu Han, a deputy mayor of Beijing, expert on the history of the Ming dynasty and author of the new edition of the chronicle play *'Hai Rui Dismissed from Office'*.

On top of that, in March 1966, Mao Zedong seriously criticised the CPC Beijing municipal committee for its 'exclusivity and lack of openness'. At the enlarged session of the political bureau of the central committee held in May, Peng Zhen was dismissed from the posts of secretary of the central committee secretariat, first secretary of the CPC Beijing municipal committee and mayor of Beijing. The CPC Beijing municipal committee was reorganised on 4 June 1966 and Wan Li was severely impacted, criticised, struggled against and paraded through the streets many times in the company of Peng Zhen and Liu Ren, the leaders in charge of the CPC Beijing municipal committee.

At the struggle meeting on 28 November 1966, Jiang Qing declared her intention to "thoroughly bring everything to light and settle accounts' and announced that 'the former CPC Beijing municipal committee, the former publicity department of the CPC central committee and the former Ministry of Culture colluded to commit monstrous crimes against the party and the people". After the meeting Wan Li was deprived of his freedom and locked up in the barracks along Wanshou road in Beijing.

Working under the leadership of Deng Xiaoping for many years, cooperating in harmony with and keeping close ties with Deng, Wan Li won the appreciation of Deng Xiaoping. They additionally shared a hobby - playing bridge (a card game). When four players showed cards in pairs, Deng Xiaoping often shouted humourously in strong Sichuan dialect that "the central committee declares war against Beijing". The revolutionary friendship was developed on the bridge table but was reduced to being the monstrous crime of forming a clique to pursue selfish interests. In the 'One Hundred Clowns Picture', Wan Li was defamed to be the sedan chair carrier and preacher of Deng Xiaoping, 'the second top dog capitalist roader in the party'. The rebels spared no efforts to discover his black ties with Deng Xiaoping.

'One Hundred Clowns Picture', a 'Cultural Revolution' caricature

Part of the 'One Hundred Clowns Picture' (the sedan chair carrier in the left corner is Wan Li)

Subjected to Criticism and Struggle with Three Model Workers on New Year's Eve

The eve of the spring festival of 1967 would normally have been a happy time for the Wan family to get together, see the old year out and ring in the new year. But a tragedy was played out in the Beijing Workers' Gymnasium - criticising and struggling against Wan Li in the company of three model workers, namely, Shi Chuanxiang, Li Ruihuan and Zhang Baifa.

Zhang Baifa was the first to be criticised and struggled against. The rebels asked him to sit on the floor rather than the stool beside him and to keep his head lowered. The second to come in, Shi Chuanxin, was a sorry sight as he looked at Zhang Baifa who was not allowed to lock up. Looking Zhang up and down, Shi Chuanxiang finally recognised him and said: "Brother, you are here as well." The warder roared: "Damn it! You still call each other brothers in jail? Get your ass over there beside the portrait of Chairman Mao hanging on the wall." At that time, they heard Li Ruihuan quarrelling with someone. In the clamour, Li Ruihuan refused to let the rebels hang a placard on him. The rebels shouted: "Behave yourself, Li Ruihuan!" The struggle meeting went on witnessed by no less than 10,000 people in the gymnasium.

Wan Li is criticised and struggled against as a 'counter-revolutionary revisionist element'

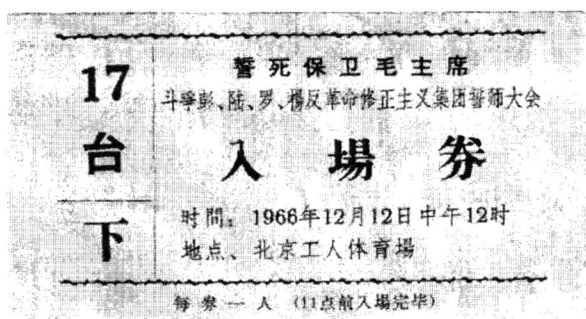

An entrance ticket to the struggle meeting in the workers' gymnasium during the 'Cultural Revolution'

Li Ruihuan and Zhang Baifa were two young shock troops who had delivered outstanding contributions to the 'national day project'; Shi Chuanxiang was a nightsoil (sewage) worker 'bringing a clean atmosphere to tens of thousands of households at the expense of the filth all around him'. Wan Li once worked as a nightsoil worker together with Shi Chuanxiang and got the nickname of the 'nightsoil mayor'. Wan Li said: "I felt the utmost joy to be criticised and struggled against on that day because I had the support of the people and was in the company of my three worker friends. How glorious that was for me!"

Before the criticism and struggle that day, Li Ruihuan said: "I was well known far and wide but will be infamous in history." Zhang Baifa added the horizontal inscription 'start from nothing'. When they told Wan Li about it, Wan Li questioned: "Why was it to 'start from nothing'? It should be 'stage a comeback'!"

When Premier Zhou received the representatives at the 10th National People's Congress (NPC) of the CPC in 1973, he said: "One nightsoil worker representative was from Chongqing and another Shi Chuanxiang was from Beijing." Premier Zhou asked where Shi Chuanxiang was. Someone answered he was being driven back to his hometown in Shandong. Premier Zhou uttered in a rage, "Isn't it ridiculous for Shi Chuanxiang to be driven back to his hometown in Shandong?! Does the Cultural Revolution plan to beat down a nightsoil worker? He should be brought back."

Although the 'Gang of Four' was still on the platform, Premier Zhou's speech spread quickly.

Subjected to Criticism and Struggle with Three Model Workers on New Year's Eve

Wan Li and Li Ruihuan

Shi Chuanxiang, a national model worker

Zhang Baifa accompanies Wan Li to inspect the Beijing railway in October 1992

At the sight of Zhang Baifa, Wan Li said: "Baifa, Premier Zhou said Shi Chuanxiang should be brought back." Then Wan Li went to tell the military representative of the environmental sanitation bureau: "Premier Zhou has instructed us to bring back Shi Chuanxiang."

The cruelly persecuted Shi Chuanxiang was brought back to Beijing and hospitalised. Wan Li was the first to see him in hospital in the company of Li Ruihuan and Zhang Baifa. Shi Chuanxiang cried bitterly but could still recognise his old friends. When Wan Li went to see him, he called him 'Mayor Wan'. Shi Chuanxiang kept crying when Wan Li was with him in the hospital.

Severely tortured in body and mind, Shi Chuanxiang unluckily passed away. In deep grief, Wan Li entrusted Bian Tao, his wife, to send Shi Chuanxiang a commemorative funeral wreath on his behalf.

Chapter 15

Blocking His Elder Sister Wan Yun's Promotion

Wan Li resumed his work in the middle stage of the 'Cultural Revolution'. When he began to work, he found many problems related to urban construction and management in Beijing. To solve these problems, he proposed to hold a meeting on urban construction and management in Beijing in June 1971 at which Wan Li delivered a speech *To Plan, Build and Manage the Capital City Well.* During 1973 and 1974, Wan Li focused on environmental protection in the capital.

Wan Li's eldest sister Wan Yun had grown up in the base area since her childhood and joined the CPC at the age of 15 under the influence of her brother. After marching into Chongqing, a vital town in the great southwest of China, together with the PLA troops, she was selected by the Communist Youth League organisation and dispatched to the Leningrad Youth League school in the Soviet Union for further study.

Wan Li resumes his work in the 'Cultural Revolution', pictured here in his house in Dingjiakeng outside Yongdingmen gate, Beijing in the winter of 1969

Wan Yun (first from left) and her family; third from left is Wan Danru

It was a special school of the Communist Party of the Soviet Union to cultivate senior cadres of the Communist Youth League. Students at the youth league school were all outstanding youths selected nationwide with war experience and would be assigned to lead communist youth leagues after graduation. The youth league school also cultivated leading cadres of the Chinese youth league for the CPC. Since they were all cadre students assigned by the state to study abroad when China and the Soviet Union were on good terms, they had a fairly high standard of living, were allocated 1,200 roubles each month as living expenses, and were treated like high-ranking cadres of the Soviet Union.

After years of study, Wan Yun graduated with excellent academic performance and was assigned to work in the central committee of the Communist Youth League. At that time, Wan Li had been transferred to work in the Beijing construction engineering department. Soon after Wan Yun took office, Wan Li talked to her and told her it wouldn't be good for her to work in a high position in the central authorities; she should work and unite with the workers and farmers in the grassroots organisations which would be good for her ideological remolding.

Due to Wan Li's intervention, Wan Yun left the central committee of the Communist Youth League, worked with the labour union of Beijing Second National Cotton Factory, and ate, lived and laboured with the workers for a long time. Working silently and delivering selfless contributions without any complaint about resigning to work in the central authorities, Wan Yun earned the respect of the workers and the trust of the party committee. Implicated along with her brother as being a member of a 'reactionary gang' in the 'Cultural Revolution' and implementing the special task entrusted by the party in the 'four clean-ups' movement, Wan Yun was criticised by name by Jiang Qing and consequently struggled against to within an inch of her life by the rebels, coming close to losing her mind. However, when she swept the toilet in the factory and the workers privately consoled and encouraged her, she unyieldingly got through it. After Wan Li regained his

Wan Li and Bian Tao in their house in Dingjiakeng outside Yongdingmen gate, Beijing in the winter of 1969

freedom, Wan Yun also resumed her work and willingly bore hard work. Through years of efforts, Wan Yun not merely resumed her former position but also gained the conditions for promotion. The leader of Beijing textile bureau went to enquire of Wan Li: "Comrade Wan Yun has done a good job and we plan to promote her to be the deputy director of the textile bureau. What's your viewpoint?"

Hearing about it, Wan Li refused immediately: "Wan Yun is not qualified. Many people are more outstanding than her and deserve promotion. Wan Yun needs to gain more practical experience."

The bureau leader highly valued Wan Li's opinion and acknowledged Wan Li's disagreement. Wan Li's sentence blocked Wan Yun's promotion. Many years later, the organisation did not ask Wan Li's opinion and directly promoted Wan Yun to be the deputy director of the bureau; she was only a bureau-level cadre when she retired.

Wan Yun in retirement chatting with famous writer Wang Meng in 2012

Chapter 16

Making a Breakthrough at Xuzhou Railway Bureau

Around the first session of the fourth NPC in early 1975, Zhou Enlai's health took a severe turn for the worse. With the backup of Mao Zedong, Deng Xiaoping successively worked as vice chairman and chief of the general staff of the central military commission, vice chairman of the central committee and first vice premier of the state council to administer the routine work of the central committee. Wan Li was appointed Minister of Railways at the first session of the fourth NPC.

Disturbed by the 'criticise Lin Biao, criticise Confucius' campaign in 1974, the volume of railway freight nationwide dropped by 5.3%, the investment in newly-built railways decreased by 3.9% over the previous year but the track-laying mileage shrank by 21.5%; the total output value of the railway industry reduced by Rmb240m over the previous year. The situation deteriorated in 1975. The whole plan was in danger of failing if the problem of railway transportation was not solved and the production and deployment were fouled up. Deng Xiaoping was firmly determined to solve that problem.

Wan Li took office in the Ministry of Railways. He saw Premier Zhou Enlai when he was walking in Beihai park. Premier Zhou asked for information about the Ministry of Railways while they were talking and Wan Li gave him a brief report on the situation. While he was talking about the chaotic and complicated situation of the railways, Premier Zhou's staffer reminded him of the time and that the premier had to leave. However, several steps away, Premier Zhou turned back telling him: "It doesn't matter. Comrade Xiaoping can work it out!"

In mid-February 1975, Comrade Xiaoping called on Gu Mu and Wan Li to talk about the problem of reorganisation in his house. He said that the railways were the lifeline of the national economy characterized by 'high, prominent, semi' (a 'high' degree of centralisation, a 'prominent' position as the main artery and 'semi'-military management) and consequently to reorganise the economy, it was necessary to start by restoring order to the railways. He clearly related the details concerned one by one, including where to start and what measures to take. Comrade Xiaoping asked them to draw up a document so that the central committee could improve railway work without further delay.

(From right): Wan Li, Deng Xiaoping, Yang Shangkun and Peng Zhen get together again after the 10 years of chaos

Less than 20 days after Wan Li took office, Deng Xiaoping called on him twice and instructed the Ministry of Railways to solve the railway problems as fast as possible to prevent the railways from dragging down the economy and the whole country. Soon afterwards, a draft was sent to the political bureau of the central committee. On 5 March 1975, the *Decision of the CPC Central Committee to Improve Railway Management* was issued to county and regiment-level units as document no. 9 of the central committee. The document chiefly carried the main contents of the decisions to improve the railway management system, to establish and complete the necessary regulatory framework, to enhance the sense of organisational discipline, to ensure safe and punctual transportation and to struggle against all sorts of disruption.

At the national meeting of party secretaries in charge of industry, the CPC Jiangsu provincial committee and the Ministry of Railways jointly wrote a report to vice premiers Wang Zhen and Gu Mu in the name of Wan Li and Xu Jiatun to propose that the CPC Jiangsu provincial committee, the Ministry of Railways and the parties concerned jointly organize a work team to solve the problems of the Xuzhou and Nanjing railway branch bureaus.

Xuzhou railway bureau was the hub station at the crossing in control of the rebels. Gu Binghua, the rebel leader of Xuzhou material administration, got his position by violence and occupied the building of the material administration. The building happened to be near the Xuzhou railway station and was a commanding elevation point. Comrade Peng Chong decided to put Gu Binghua in prison, which created favourable conditions for Wan Li to eliminate the problem of Xuzhou branch bureau.

The reorganisation started by studying and publicising the document. On 10 March, the second day after Wan Li's arrival in Xuzhou, a conference attended by 10,000 people including all the workers and family members of Xuzhou railway branch bureau was held to convey the spirit of the central committee document no. 9, at which Wan Li passed on the central committee document and Deng Xiaoping's speech in person. On 11 March, a mobilisation meeting was held for party members from Xuzhou city and Xuzhou area; on 13 March, a mass rally was held with the participation of all the staff and workers of the railway locomotive branch to ensure smooth railway operation.

Xuzhou railway branch bureau suffered some problems during these years due to the disruption of gangsters. First, factionalism was serious.

The ideology of factionalism prevailed among cadres and workers. The two factions were well defined. Not only did the workers choose to join different factions but the leaders of all levels had similar problems to varying degrees and drew the line in work according to their factions; second, the aftermath of the so-called '16 May' elements among some cadres and workers was not appropriately handled, which affected the mood and enthusiasm for work among them, their families and friends; third, the rules and regulations ceased to be binding, organisational discipline was slack, the tasks of transportation and production could not be completed for a long time and accidents occurred constantly.

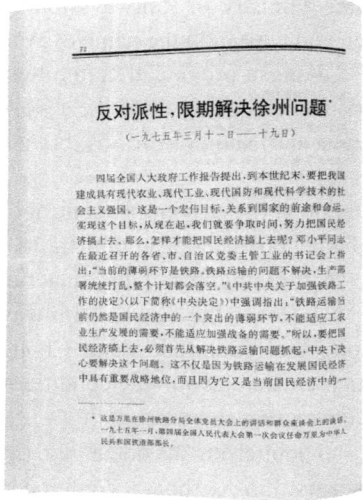

Wan Li's speech at the Xuzhou railway branch bureau that year entitled *Oppose Factionalism and Promptly Resolve the Xuzhou Problem* - 11-19 March 1975

Wan Li did not simply talk about these problems at the meetings, big and small, but also went deep among the grassroots work teams and groups. He pinpointed that the problems of Xuzhou primarily rested in serious factionalism which destroyed stability and unity, transportation and production, and had a harmful impact on industrial and agricultural production and people's lives. A minority of the rebel leaders taking the lead in making trouble were 'seriously criticised, dismissed from office or transferred from their former units'. Anyone disobeying the transfer would not be paid. Those who were incorrigibly obstinate, went their own way in factionalism and violated the law were brought to justice.

Wan Li predominantly supervised the reorganisation of the leading group of the branch bureau. He personally chaired the CPC bureau committee meeting and listened to the reports and self-criticism of the standing committee members one by one. Wan Li patiently and meticulously conducted ideological work, did not interrupt the standing committee members when they talked but only gave affirmation or criticism practically and realistically. He strictly criticised the elements and issues stirring up factionalism, adhered to the principle of changing ideology rather than posts, adjusted some individual cadres and transferred a standing committee member of the CPC bureau committee whose mind was seriously affected by factionalism and invited serious complaints to be addressed to the president of the Jinan Railway Bureau Party School.

The Xuzhou railway branch bureau shunting yard

Wan Li emphasised that the central committee document no.9 clearly shows you the direction and that the higher-level leaders are taking responsibility for you. Now you are only required to walk tall, criticise factionalism, strengthen party character and lead cadres of all levels and all workers to turn the situation around and take on a new look before late March. He hoped that Xuzhou branch bureau would change from being backward to being advanced and take a strong lead in the national railway system.

Wan Li, the CPC Jiangsu provincial committee and the CPC Xuzhou municipal committee quickened the pace of rehabilitation arising from the '16 May' issue arousing drastic complaints among the people, properly handled the aftermath, concurrently rebuilt all sorts of rules and regulations, established and completed the post responsibility system, the technical operation specification and the quality inspection system, and formulated methods of punishment for accidents resulting from violation of rules and regulations.

Wan Li inspects the Xinxiang-Heze railway in November 1985; second from left in the front row is Yao Yilin

Wan Li stayed in Xuzhou for 10 days and the work team of the Ministry of Railways worked continuously until April. Through reorganisation, the mental outlook of the cadres and people of the Xuzhou railway branch bureau and the Xuhai area changed and the production situation took a rapid turn for the better. By 20 March, the number of trains deployed on the line rose from the previous 38 to 72, that of the locomotives dispatched soared from the previous 70 to 90 and that of the loaded carriages increased from more than 200 to more than 1,400 every day on average. In April, the situation of transportation and production of the Xuzhou railway branch bureau took a turn for the better, completing the monthly production plan three days in advance and ending the chaotic situation whereby the production plan had not been completed for 21 months in a row. Xuzhou also brought an end to the chaotic situation. Its industrial output value grew by 3.2% in April and by 36% in the first half of May over the same period of the previous year.

Wan Li goes into Dayaoshan tunnel to inspect the construction of the tunnel face in December 1985

Chapter 17

Going to Zhengzhou Railway Bureau Three Times to Tackle Thorny Issues

Wan Li returned to Beijing on 22 March 1975 and reported to the State Council the information concerning the passing on and implementation of the central committee's document no. 9 to solve the problems in Xuzhou on 25 March 1975.

Deng Xiaoping highly valued his summary of the Xuzhou railway reorganisation. He said, after the central committee's document no. 9 was issued, railway transportation immediately took a turn for the better and greatly influenced and promoted the development of all trades. Their main experience was to develop production by means of freely mobilising people and conducting persistent struggles against factionalism. The railway department did well in that respect and Xuzhou's experience was comparatively typical and worth studying. The railway department also had to hold a meeting to check the implementation of document no. 9 and summarise the experience. Resolute measures had to be taken against units indulging in factionalism which had to be eradicated within the prescribed time without any delay.

In mid-April, Wan Li came to Zhengzhou railway bureau to explain and publicise the essence of the central committee's document no. 9 and mobilise the people to criticise factionalism. He demanded that Zhengzhou railway bureau take measures and promptly change the passive situation of eratic railway transportation.

Zhengzhou railway bureau was the hub of the national railway transportation system but was often blocked and had been chaotic in the 'Cultural Revolution'. During January through October 1974, Zhengzhou railway bureau underloaded coal on 273 trains every day on average, 68 serious accidents occurred, the punctuality rate of goods train operations was merely 57.9% and the task of transportation was not finished for five months. On new year's day 1975, the Beijing-Guangzhou railway line was blocked, which affected transportation nationwide. There was an extremely urgent need to reorganise Zhengzhou railway bureau.

Nonetheless, Tang Qishan, a gangster in the main leadership of Zhengzhou railway bureau, was a member of the 10th central committee, standing committee member of the CPC Henan provincial committee, secretary of the CPC Zhengzhou municipal committee and secretary of the CPC Zhengzhou railway bureau committee. He and his accomplices overtly agreed but covertly opposed, expressed their determination to implement the central committee's decision and develop railway transportation at full speed to Wan Li's face. After Wan Li's delegation left Henan, they did the opposite, spread rumours against the reorganisation of the Ministry of Railways and messed up Zhengzhou railway bureau. In May 1975, Zhengzhou railway bureau did not complete the task of transportation, the punctuality rate of goods train operations was merely 64.7% and serious accidents happened constantly.

That being the case, Wan Li transferred Su Hua from Lanzhou railway bureau to be the second secretary of Zhengzhou railway bureau to strengthen the leadership capability. In early June, Wan Li headed a work team to Henan for the second time. On 3 June, Wan Li announced in Xinxiang the removal of gangster Xing Jiejiang from the posts of deputy secretary of the CPC Xinxiang branch bureau committee and deputy director of the revolutionary committee, and appointed leader Liang Zhijie to replace him as secretary of the branch bureau party committee and director of the revolutionary committee. The decision was warmly applauded by the railway workers, there was a crackdown on the gangster forces and this immediately turned around the situation of the Xinxiang branch bureau.

The first secretary of the CPC Zhengzhou railway bureau committee was an old comrade who had worked with Wan Li in the Hebei-Shandong-Henan area. Unexpectedly, he stood on the side of the gangsters. At the bureau party committee meeting during 4-9 June, he questioned Wan Li and held the view that the gangster Xing Jiejiang should not be dealt with by the Ministry of Railways. He thought that the experience in reorganising

Xuzhou railway bureau was not suitable for Zhengzhou railway bureau and that Wan Li's criticism of Zhengzhou railway bureau did not conform with the reality. Furthermore, Tang Qishan and the others did not admit their factionalism and mistakes at all. The two different ways of thinking were argued tit for tat in an intense struggle. Wan Li tried to persuade that secretary: "We are old partners. My sincere opinion was aimed at helping you." Unexpectedly, the secretary responded: "There is no leeway in the struggle between different lines." The contrasting feelings were at a complete stalemate.

On 10 June, Wan Li resolutely reorganised the leading group of Zhengzhou railway bureau, dismissed the former first secretary of the bureau party committee from the railway system and appointed Su Hua to administer the party committee as the first secretary of the CPC Zhengzhou railway bureau committee and Hu Yiping to administer the revolutionary committee of the bureau. These resolute measures vigorously attacked the overbearing attitude of the gang of Tang Qishan, stimulated the enthusiasm of the railway workers to throw themselves into transportation and production, and changed the transportation situation of Zhengzhou railway bureau for the better at a stroke.

But the gang of Tang Qishan was not reconciled to lose. With the connivance of the main leaders of the provincial party committee, they began to counterattack, obstinately resisted the decision of the central committee and the instructions of the Ministry of Railways, charged Wan Li's handling of the problems at Zhengzhou railway bureau as 'instigating factionalism', 'attacking new cadres' and 'destroying stability and unity', blatantly smeared the central committee's document no.9 as a 'regressive programme' and incited everywhere that 'it would be victory to drag down transportation and production'. Tang Qishan instigated someone else to compile a 'collection of Wan Li's words' and repeatedly reported fabricated crimes of Wan Li and Su Hua to the 'Gang of Four'. The fearful disruption of the gangsters enormously disturbed the reorganisation of Zhengzhou railway bureau and some units were still in a chaotic state. In July 1975, Zhengzhou railway bureau was still underloaded by more than 10,000 trains of coal.

The CPC central committee and the State Council paid much attention to the situation of Zhengzhou railway bureau. On 24 July, the leaders of the central committee including Li Xiannian, Hua Guofeng, Wu De, Wan Li and Liu Jianxun, who was the first secretary of the CPC Henan provincial committee, listened to the report of Su Hua, Tang Qishan and Hu Yiping on the work of Zhengzhou railway bureau. After listening to the report, Li Xiannian clearly affirmed the correct solution to the problem of the leading group of Zhengzhou railway bureau and stressed the need to promptly implement the 'three instructions' of Chairman Mao and the central committee's document no. 9 so as to develop railway transportation to a higher degree; to investigate and deal with the people and issues destroying railway transportation accordingly and take strict measures to deal with behaviour that overstepped the mark. He also decided to have Vice Premier Ji Dengkui take the lead and join hands with the Ministry of Railways and the CPC Henan provincial committee in a bid to work out the reorganisation of Zhengzhou railway bureau.

In late July 1975, Wan Li headed for Henan for the third time and

Wan Li (second from right), vice minister of railways Deng Cunlun (second from left) and others investigating the Anhui-Jiangxi railway in November 1977

In 1984, Wan Li investigates the newly-built Yanzhou-Shijiusuo railway

In 1986, Wan Li investigates Anhui Wuhu railway station

discussed with the CPC Henan provincial committee how to solve the problem of Zhengzhou railway bureau. On 1 August 1975, Ji Dengkui attended an enlarged standing committee meeting of the Zhengzhou railway bureau committee, strictly criticised the figures stirring up factionalism and announced the establishment of a work group headed by Liu Jianxun and Wan Li to be jointly responsible for reorganising Zhengzhou railway bureau.

The railway system launched overall reorganisation in 1975 which made the Tianjin railway line a busy scene. The picture shows workers loading and transporting construction materials at the western freight yard of the Tianjin railway station

The established work group mobilised railway workers to intensively bring to light and criticise the words and deeds of the gangsters damaging railway transportation, removed a group of gangsters from their duties, adjusted and strengthened the leading groups of Zhengzhou, Luoyang, Xinxiang and Xinyang branch bureaus and transferred the gangster leaders destroying reorganisation and railway transportation from their former units or posts according to the instructions of Deng Xiaoping 'to transfer or dismiss the gangster leaders whenever they arise'.

These resolute measures made it possible for Zhengzhou railway bureau to be reorganised and the situation of production and transportation was able to take a turn for the better day by day. In early August, central and southern Henan encountered catastrophic flooding and more than 100km of railway lines in the central part of the Beijing-Guangzhou railway in Henan were destroyed with the downstream line cut off for 18 days and the upstream line for 46 days. The railway workers energetically fought the floods and provided relief, made urgent repairs on the railway and transported relief supplies day and night. By late September, they had transported more than 20,000 trains of materials to fight the floods and provide relief to the disaster-stricken areas. In the case whereby flooding caused enormous destruction to railway transportation, Zhengzhou railway bureau fought in unity and the main economic and technical indicators of the whole bureau registered a comprehensive upward trend. Daily average coal movements of the entire bureau increased by 267 trains and the number of trains picking up and delivering goods grew by 30% in November compared with September. Transportation and production basically recovered to their pre-flooding level.

What's worth mentioning is that during the period when Wan Li reorganised Zhengzhou railway bureau as the minister of railways, his first daughter-in-law was working in Zhengzhou (Henan) railway bureau. Someone warm-hearted hoped to help his first daughter-in-law to transfer to work in Beijing railway bureau with her child by way of the organisation to solve the practical difficulty that the couple lived in separate places. Everything was done except for an imminent transfer order.

Wan Bo'ao and his wife lived in separate places

Going to Zhengzhou Railway Bureau Three Times to Tackle Thorny Issues

Wan Bo'ao and his daughter Yangyang

Just then, a vice minister of railways told Wan Li, minister of railways, when he made a work report to him: "We're planning to transfer your daughter-in-law from Zhengzhou railway bureau to Beijing railway bureau in a bid to end the days of the couple living in separate places."

At this, Wan Li refuted resolutely and decisively, "Isn't it good to work in Zhengzhou railway bureau? How come she will be transferred to work in Beijing? Who will do the work in Zhengzhou if everyone is transferred to Beijing? They are not the only couple living in separate places. Similar problems affecting others should be worked out first. I don't agree to her transfer and anyone transferring her is making a mistake."

A sentence from Wan Li shattered his first daughter-in-law's wonderful dream of working in Beijing. After working in Zhengzhou for years, his first daughter-in-law tried her own means to transfer to Shenzhen, worked and settled down there and was never transferred to Beijing even to this day.

Chapter 18

No Choice But to Sign After Being Singled Out by Hua Guofeng

In the short-term railway reorganisation that lasted just over three months, the problem of traffic congestion at all the stations and depots was basically resolved. During those three months, Deng Xiaoping conducted all-round reorganisation and the nationwide situation fundamentally took a turn for the better. However, Mao Zedong did not allow Deng Xiaoping to rectify the 'cultural revolution'. On 20 November 1975, the political bureau of the central committee discussed the evaluation of the 'cultural revolution' according to the views of Mao Zedong and wrongly criticised Deng Xiaoping. Mao Zedong proposed to have Deng Xiaoping make a resolution to affirm the 'cultural revolution' with the general evaluation of '30% shortcomings and 70% achievements'. Deng Xiaoping tactfully declined, saying: "It's not proper for me to draft the resolution because I am detached from the situation (literally "because I am a peach blossom among people, unaware of the ways of the Han, let alone the Wei and the Jin" (dynasties))."

After that, criticism of Deng Xiaoping gradually escalated. In late November, the 'counterattack on the rightist reversal of verdicts' campaign was launched countrywide, interrupting nine consecutive months of rectification work, and the areas all over the country where the rectification work had been most prominent were the hardest hit by the 'rightist reversal of verdicts' campaign. Some rebel leaders and cadres punished in the rectification took the lead in criticising the 'rightist reversal of verdicts' campaign of the Ministry of Railways with the support of the main provincial party committee leaders.

Lanzhou and Zhengzhou railway bureaus were the first to make trouble.

Some rebel leaders in the Lanzhou railway bureau besieged and detained Li Guang, the working group leader of the Ministry of Railways in Lanzhou and director of the ministry's political department. Factionalism revived in the Zhengzhou railway bureau and the leading group's ability to continue functioning was paralysed. Transportation and production plummeted and it was impossible to load and unload trains in Zhengzhou railway station where the number of trains stranded accounted for half of all the trains on the network. The Zhengzhou railway terminal was blocked, endangering the whole system and causing a severe blockage!

Deng Xiaoping struggled head-to-head with 'the gang of four' when he was running the day-to-day affairs of the central committee in 1975 and started to carry out all-round rectification so that the national situation fundamentally changed for the better

For this reason, the central committee had to urgently summon the main leading cadres of Henan and Gansu provinces, and of the Zhengzhou and Lanzhou railway bureaus, to Beijing to resolve the problem. Xian Henghan, the first secretary of the CPC Gansu provincial committee, Liu Jianxun, the first secretary and Tang Qishan, the secretary of the CPC Henan provincial committee respectively came to Beijing in late January in the company of others.

As instructed by Hua Guofeng, the makeshift leading group of the Ministry of Railways began to listen to the views and criticism of the main leading cadres of Henan and Gansu provinces, and of the Zhengzhou and Lanzhou railway bureaus respectively from 21 January. The main leaders of the two provincial party committees originally expressed their 'agreement' and 'support' when the problems of the two bureaus were dealt with the year before. Especially, when the problem of Zhengzhou railway bureau was handled, the main leaders of the CPC Henan provincial committee Liu Jianxun and Tang Qishan voiced their viewpoint to the central committee leaders. Sensing the trend of events was different, they utterly forgot what they had just said and blatantly changed their views to say that "they had been boycotting and opposed to it". Liu Jianxun and Tang Qishan surprisingly wrote in the position paper that "the provincial party committee was totally opposed to what the Ministry of Railways and Su Hua did and had pointed it out repeatedly". Xian Henghan also wrote down in the position paper that "the provincial party committee was opposed to it and the Ministry of Railways should be fully responsible for it".

In 1975, Wan Li went by train to conduct an investigation visit. Wan Li is pictured here (front row, sixth from right) with local leaders when they visited the former residence of Comrade Mao Zedong in Shaoshan

No Choice But to Sign After Being Singled Out by Hua Guofeng

In drafting the documents to resolve the problems of the Zhengzhou and Lanzhou railway bureaus, the leaders of the Ministry of Railways, including Wan Li and Li Xin, took the view that if the Ministry of Railways admitted the rectification mistakes of the two bureaus, it was the equivalent of negating document no.9 of the central committee. But on the condition that the central committee leaders instructed the Ministry of Railways to 'unify their ideology and views with those of the provincial party committee', Wan Li's viewpoint was of little importance. Even so, Wan Li still firmly refused to write down the name of Su Hua, the first deputy secretary of the CPC Zhengzhou railway bureau committee and Li Guang, the political department director of the Ministry of Railways, in the documents. He said: "They were dispatched by us and implemented our decision. I should assume the responsibility for the mistakes and my name should be included. It was entirely my idea. I won't sign it if you disagree."

The stalemate lasted for another week. On the evening of 9 February, the State Council leaders including Hua Guofeng and Ji Dengkui called in Wan Li and Li Xin. Hua Guofeng criticised them for the delay in solving the problems in Lanzhou and Zhengzhou. As to the question of names in the documents, Ji Dengkui said in embarrassment that: "Your idea and requirement are understandable. But the central committee should decide the name to be written. You can have reservations about your disagreement." Consequently, Wan Li had to obey the central committee's decision and had no alternative but to sign his name on the documents.

After 'the Gang of Four' was smashed, Hua Guofeng was assigned to be the chairman of the CPC central committee and the Central Military Commission and continued to be premier of the State Council

On the evening of 14 February, Hua Guofeng, Wang Hongwen, Ji Dengkui and Wu De called in the leaders of the CPC Henan and Gansu provincial committees, the makeshift leading group members and the leaders in charge of the Zhengzhou and Lanzhou railway bureaus. Hua Guofeng delivered a speech on behalf of the CPC central committee and the leaders of the State Council. After the interview, all the makeshift leading group members of the Ministry of Railways attending the meeting were detained, instructed and criticised separately.

In December 1983, Wan Li fastened the last bolt for the track-laying and connection of the electrified Beijing-Qinhuangdao multiple-track railway. Hu Qili is the fourth from left in the back row

Hua Guofeng criticised: First, you (Wan Li) made many mistakes. For instance, you spoke of "four types of chaos - ideological chaos, organisational chaos, team chaos and institutional chaos"; you took factionalism as the main conflict and you made mistakes about the situation, taking a minor issue to be the main trend; the primary responsibility did not rest with you but Deng Xiaoping; you dared in the past, and should dare now, to do whatever is instructed by Chairman Mao and to assume responsibility and criticise the 'rightist reversal of verdicts' campaign. The leading group of the ministry should on the one hand examine their mistakes and on the other hand criticise Deng Xiaoping, examine which aspects of Deng Xiaoping's line you have implemented and draw a line under it. Comrade Wan Li, you should change your attitude. Second, you refused to write down the names of Li Guang and Su Hua in the documents. The ministry and the provincial committee hold different views on that. Gansu provincial committee called back Li Guang for the purpose of facilitating the work. Li Guang and Su Hua can stay here and return sometime later after their problems have been resolved.

The 25 days of fierce struggles dealing with the problems of the Zhengzhou and Lanzhou railway bureaus finally ended with the 'victory' of Liu Jianxun and Tang Qishan.

Chapter 19

Thousands of People Petition the Ministry of Railways

In late February 1976, the central committee's documents on solving the problems of the Zhengzhou and Lanzhou railway bureaus were issued and ignited the flames of the Ministry of Railways' campaign to 'criticise Deng Xiaoping and counterattack the rightist reversal of verdicts'.

A 10-metre-high couplet was pasted on the ground floor of the Ministry of Railways office building, with the top line reading: 'Treat the rebels with disdain', while the bottom line read: 'Willingly serving for the restoration of a dethroned monarch' and the top of the poster read: 'Always doing alike'. Slogans such as 'Ferret out the capitalist roader and main accomplice Wan Li', 'Ferret out Wan Li, a pioneer of Deng Xiaoping negating the cultural revolution', 'Wan Li deserves death for his crime of suppressing the rebels' and 'The trains will not run unless Wan Li is toppled' were written on the walls of the courtyard.

Some petitioners came to Beijing from the subordinate units of the railway system and assaulted the institutions of the Ministry of Railways. Most of the petitioners were rebel leaders or cadres and workers kept in the dark and punished or criticised in the rectification of the railway system in 1975. Male or female, some with children, they rushed everywhere aggressively and unreasonably. They wanted to see Wan Li, Liu Jianzhang (vice minister of railways and department party committee secretary) by name and the working group leaders concerned.

Wan Li and Liu Jianzhang spent more than a week receiving petitioners from the Taiyuan and Linfen branch bureaus, Lanzhou first railway design institute, Lanzhou railway bureau, Luoyang locomotive works and Kunming railway bureau, listened to their 'opinions' and 'criticism', publicised the policies to them and mobilised them to return to their former units to join the revolution and production. Their efforts had little effect and some returned and then came back. The chain reaction, which Wan Li feared most, finally appeared. More and more petitioners came and made trouble increasingly violently. They did not want to see other leaders but wanted to see Wan Li and Liu Jianzhang detained, wanted to wage a 'wheel war' against them and to besiege them so that the leaders of the ministry could not work there and the leading group meeting could not be held in the department but in the no. 27 theatre. To cope with that situation, Vice Minister Liu Jianzhang could not attend the leading group meeting but specially received the petitioners.

More and more petitioners came to Beijing, with the numbers peaking at more than 400 per day. The guesthouse of the Ministry of Railways was not spacious enough to accommodate them so some petitioners had to live outside it. The number of petitioners was directly related to the support of the local provincial committee leaders. The leaders in charge of the CPC Jiangsu provincial committee were not supportive of petitioning, so few petitioners came from Jiangsu. By contrast, the leaders in charge of the CPC Gansu and Henan provincial committees applauded the petitioners, so more petitioners came from these two provinces and the petitioners said they made the petition with the overt support of some leaders. Petitioners from units affiliated with the Lanzhou railway bureau made the greatest scene. Dozens of them occupied Wan Li's office, stationed themselves there, wanted to see Wan Li every day, ate and stayed there, and besieged and tussled with him. Long-distance calls to all corners of the country could be made in the ministers' offices. Consequently, Wan Li's and Liu Jianzhang's offices became their 'liaison office'.

At noon on 6 March, Zhang Guangyou, a Xinhua News Agency correspondent stationed in the ministry offices, came to the office of the ministry. Zhang Genming in the duty room invited him to Wan Li's office. Opening the door, Zhang Guangyou unexpectedly saw petitioners, male and female, were crowded in there, some even with children. It was noon break then and the petitioners lay on the floor, on the sofa, in the bed, on the desk, chairs and even on the windowsills. 'Down with Wan Li' was inscribed on the walls of the office.

Wan Li wrote an inscription praising Liu Jianzhang in 2009

More than 40 petitioners from Kunming railway bureau took Wan Li to the conference building (the guesthouse of the Ministry of Railways) on 11 March. Wan Li's secretaries Yu Lian and Xu Shouhe sensed the situation was getting out of hand and told correspondent Zhang Guangyou: "The petitioners from Kunming railway bureau may find fault with Comrade Wan Li today. You should go and take a look. Even if you keep silent, they will feel deterred and constrained. If necessary, you can persuade them, exercise your role and rescue Comrade Wan Li from the siege in your capacity as a correspondent."

Wan Li and Yu Qiuli at a meeting with all the representatives attending the National Progressive Railway Production Representatives Assembly in the Great Hall of the People in November 1982

Therefore, Zhang Guangyou and Huang Fengchu, another Xinhua News Agency correspondent, accompanied Wan Li to a simple bungalow in the conference building of the Ministry of Railways. With some benches around the walls, the room of about 70 to 80sqm was crowded with 40 or 50 men ablaze with ferocious anger.

A leader of the petitioners began to raise questions in an increasingly intense and aggressive way and did not stop until 1:30pm. Zhang Guangyou rose to urge them: "It's past one o'clock and it's time for lunch." They refused and said: "We haven't finished." Zhang responded: "You should let him and yourselves have lunch. What time is it? You can continue after lunch!" Drawing Wan Li out of the room, he said: "If you can't find him, come and look for me!"

In May 1987, Wan Li visited the engineering and technical staff participating in railway construction and inspected the work at the breakthrough point in the Dayaoshan tunnel

Chapter 20

Hospitalised for Treatment Due to Continuous Tussles

Wan Li and Zhang Guangyou had lunch at Wan Li's. After lunch, they sat on the sofa in the lounge drinking tea. Wan Li briefed Zhang Guangyou concerning his viewpoint about the Ministry of Railways. Wan Li said: "Everyone unanimously agreed with and applauded the rectification of the railways last year which yielded noticeable results. Was there any flaw or mistake? It was inevitable in some aspects but not the problem of any individual. What I'm worried about is not my personal gain or loss but the impact on transportation and production. Now they are targeting Deng Xiaoping as a matter of fact. Everything will go smoothly if Deng Xiaoping is not toppled. Otherwise, it's useless for you to defend me. I can't understand it. But it is an objective fact."

When it came to the swarms of petitioners, Wan Li's view was that "it is extremely complicated. Last year the Ministry of Railways took the lead in the overall rectification, criticised factionalism and rectified the leading groups of some units. The petitioners came to make a scene mainly for the purpose of reversing the verdicts on themselves, taking advantage of the 'criticise Deng Xiaoping and counterattack the rightist reversal of verdicts' campaign. Their intentions are proved by mountains of facts. The most petitioners stirring up the greatest turmoil are from the Lanzhou and Zhengzhou railway bureaus, publicly saying they are backed by certain leaders who clearly are inciting the petitioners with the aim of crippling the institutions of the Ministry of Railways and usurping the leadership of the ministry."

In reality, the struggle for the leadership of the Ministry of Railways had begun in early 1976. At that time, Sun Jian, vice premier of the state council in charge of railways, invited Guo Lu, vice minister of railways in rehabilitation in Tianjin, to reorganise the production management team directly in the charge of Sun Jian with the excuse that railway transportation could not be suspended with Wan Li kept in the dark.

The returning Vice Minister Guo positively participated in the struggles in the 'criticise Deng Xiaoping and counterattack the rightist reversal of verdicts' campaign. He primarily supported the petitioners who were dissatisfied with the railway ministry rectification and held that the petitioners were "the victims of Wan Li's implementation of Deng Xiaoping's wrong line" and that "Wan Li had been 'invited' to implement Deng Xiaoping's wrong line", and in addition that Wan Li "deserved it", "asked for trouble" and "reaped what he had sown'.

Wan Li was cruelly persecuted and struggled against in the 'Cultural Revolution'; the poster round his neck reads: 'Counter-revolutionary revisionist element Wan Li'

He reorganised the working team, controlled the leadership of the campaign and made brief reports contrary to the facts to the central committee and the grassroots organisations. Wan Li said: "I never said anything involving my attitude toward Chairman Mao as reported. If I had signed my name, wouldn't it have been equivalent to an admission of guilt?"

At the next meeting, the leaders including Vice Minister Guo agreed Wan Li could make necessary modifications in accordance with the facts. Wan Li's modifications were checked, approved and reported to the State Council leaders. It was originally a fairly routine matter. But Guo Lu informed the State Council leaders secretly and hid it from Wan Li, casting a veil over the background and process of modifications to the brief report, distorting the facts, making trouble and causing Ji Dengkui and Sun Jian to stringently criticise Wan Li. Afterwards, the leading group of the ministry held a meeting to criticise Wan Li in accordance with the criticism by Ji Dengkui and Sun Jian. It was indeed rare to see a criticism meeting with such a strident tone and such a tense atmosphere.

Due to serious infections brought about by continuous criticism and struggle, one of Wan Li's legs was swollen and one was emaciated. The doctor said: "The infections may lead to amputation and even death." But Wan Li responded: "It's not proper to be hospitalised now. Otherwise, there would be gossip that I tried to shirk the struggle."

Wan Li was not hospitalised in Beijing hospital until 15 June. But the 'gang of four' and its followers did not give up criticising and struggling against Wan Li. On 20 June, Sun Jian came to the hospital in person and announced the decision of the central committee that "Guo Lu should take charge of the Ministry of Railways" and Wan Li should "examine and clarify the problems". The Ministry of Railways set up a special group to examine Wan Li's case.

Guo Lu energetically planned and prepared for the mass meeting to criticise and struggle against Wan Li. The first one occurred on 27 July when he sent someone to the hospital to inform Wan Li that he should make a self-criticism at a meeting of the whole ministry the next day. But it happened that the Tangshan earthquake occurred at dawn the next day and the meeting did not happen. The second time occurred on 8 September when he did the same thing but Chairman Mao passed away the next day. The meeting was postponed once again. When he scheduled it for the third time on 6 October, the 'gang of four' collapsed that day.

Wan Li was toppled for the second time in the 'counterattacking the rightist reversal of verdicts' campaign in 1976. The photo shows Wan Li's wife Bian Tao in front of Tiananmen square in September 1976 to deeply mourn Chairman Mao Zedong

Bian Tao later said: "You see, what a coincidence! He had three narrow escapes. It was probably Wan Li's destiny that he touched god."

Between the torture of being criticised and driven out of office, Wan Li, together with all other Chinese, was greatly saddened by a series of blows when Premier Zhou passed away, Deng Xiaoping was driven out of office, Zhu De passed away, Tangshan was hit by an earthquake and Chairman Mao passed away.

In May, disaster befell Wan Li's family. Wan Li's mother was seriously ill. He was criticised and struggled against every day and could not attend to his bed-ridden mother nor tell her anything about it. Wan Li was the only son of his family of origin. After he threw himself into the revolution, his mother took on sole responsibility for the heavy burden of looking after the family, positively supported and worked silently and diligently for the revolution. After liberation, Wan Li took her up to Beijing and she did most of the housework.

People in the capital swarmed into the streets to celebrate victory in smashing the 'gang of four' in October 1976; the words on the poster read: 'Overthrow the anti-party clique of Wang Hongwen, Zhang Chunqiao, Jiang Qing and Yao Wenyuan'

Wan Li felt extremely anxious. Actually, his mother understood very well what was on his mind. She asked her second grandson: "What's wrong with the train operating on schedule?" Wan Zhongxiang responded: "People would rather live a rough socialist life than a prosperous capitalist one."

At about 2am on 11 May, Wan Li's mother asked the nurses to call Wan Li and his wife to her sickbed. With Wan Li's hand in hers, the ordinary but great mother passed away in a perplexed and anxious state.

Chapter 21

Cutting Through the Chaos to Solve the Cover-up in Anhui

In April 1977, Wan Li was transferred to be the first deputy director of the department of light industry and secretary of the party leadership group. In June, he inspected the work in Yingkou. A central committee asked Wan Li to return to Beijing as soon as possible. A staffer from the department of light industry found him in an apple orchard on Yingkou farm via the duty room of the Ministry of Railways. The news spread like wildfire and hundreds of Yingkou railway workers spontaneously went to see off their old minister at the railway station.

Deng Xiaoping and Wan Li talk at Deng's home

Wan Li, Gu Zhuoxin and Zhao Shouyi attend the welcome party of the CPC Anhui provincial committee on 25 June 1977

People from all walks of life in Anhui hold a celebration parade to firmly uphold the CPC central committee's decision to solve the problems in Anhui

When Wan Li returned to Beijing, the central committee decided to appoint him to be the second secretary of the CPC Hubei provincial committee. Before his departure, he visited Deng Xiaoping to say goodbye to his old boss. Deng Xiaoping was free to move around at that stage but did not appear in public. Hearing that Wan Li was going to work in Hubei, he hesitated for a moment and said: "Don't rush to go. You should wait for a few days." Deng Xiaoping suggested that the central committee leaders send an experienced troubleshooter to solve the 'prolonged difficulties'. A couple of days later, on 22 June, the central committee decided to appoint Wan Li as the first secretary of the CPC Anhui provincial committee, director of the Anhui provincial revolutionary committee and the first political commissar of the Anhui provincial military region.

In late 1976, there were various stories going around about Wan Li's appointment. Wan Li once asked Deng Xiaoping who responded: "I am bogged down trying to cross the river and unable even to fend for myself, let alone you". Nonetheless, only six months later, before Deng Xiaoping officially resumed work, he appointed Wan Li to work in Anhui, which was later seen to be a breakthrough in China's reforms. The seemingly random arrangement was actually a judicious strategic move.

Anhui historically had been a disaster-plagued agricultural province. In the 'cultural revolution', Anhui was a province where the army was stationed early on. The army stationed in Anhui registered enormous achievements in 1967 in curbing the armed struggles between the mass organisations of two factions, stablised the situation in Anhui and was praised by Mao Zedong. After that, up to 1,000 army cadres were appointed as leaders at all levels in Anhui. That situation led the leaders of Anhui to mistakenly believe that Anhui was special. Not only did they not proactively mobilise people to expose and criticise the wrongdoing of the 'gang of four' but they also boycotted investigation of people and issues related to the 'gang of four' and kept them secret for more than eight months so that the campaign in Anhui to expose and criticise the 'gang of four' was quietly put on the backburner leading to the stagnation of industrial and agricultural production.

Wan Li was well aware of the special situation in Anhui. He immediately applied to the central committee for its decision, adopted the first resolute measure and swiftly withdrew all the army cadres 'supporting the leftists'.

At the leaders' conference to convey the central committee's instructions, Wan Li emphasised that the army cadres 'supporting the leftists' sent to Anhui in the 'cultural revolution' had made positive contributions and made significant achievements in difficult circumstances. As the situation developed and changed, the tasks were successfully finished and there was no need for army cadres to stay in the local area. The central committee decided that, except for special circumstances, in principle all army cadres should be transferred to do army work. All the units were obliged to go ahead and take their leave. They were not allowed to hold on tight and not let go, to be criticised or struggled against. Any dissent could be reported to provincial party committee leaders.

Cutting Through the Chaos to Solve the Cover-up in Anhui

Leaders including Wan Li (third from left) join in a celebration parade to show their support for the central committee's correct decision to solve the problems in Anhui

Wan Li said: "I believe the army stationed in Anhui has delivered meritorious military service. I'm sure it will carry forward the glorious revolutionary traditions and continue to play its role in supporting and helping work in the local area."

Thanks to the effective, timely ideological, organisational and unification work of the provincial party committee leaders, people in many areas of Anhui enthusiastically sent cadres 'supporting the leftists' back to the army. Up to 1,000 cadres 'supporting the leftists' throughout the province withdrew in just five days.

The leading group of the CPC Anhui provincial committee totalled 15 members consisting of three different elements. Five of them, comprising one third, were military cadres 'supporting the leftists'. Their withdrawal facilitated one third of the work to be completed by the leading group of the provincial party committee. Another third, totalling five people, included educated youths selected from the 'cultural revolution' and 'people's representatives'. Wan Li made a resolute decision to transfer all of them to work in grassroots units without any exception. In that way, that one third of work was well managed.

Wan Li making a speech dealing with the rehabilitation of unjust, false and erroneous cases at a conference held in Jianghuai theatre in Hefei for literary and art workers in 1978

After the two groups of people left the leading positions in the provincial party committee, all the people and issues implicated with the 'gang of four' were revealed. Wan Li clearly supported people to expose and criticise the wrongdoing of some typical influential leaders with serious problems and a bad attitude in the institutions under the provincial party committee. The people's enthusiasm was mobilised at once, which streamlined the investigations.

Cutting Through the Chaos to Solve the Cover-up in Anhui

Wan Li investigates Hefei steel works in the spring of 1978

The last third concerned the old cadres. Wan Li revamped two-thirds of the provincial committee leading group. He spent six months visiting most cities and counties throughout the province. Whenever he came to a place, Wan Li would take out the name list of the cadres before the 'cultural revolution' and make inquiries one by one: Where are the former secretary, deputy secretary, commissioners and deputy commissioners of the prefectural party committee? Where are the former secretary of the county party committee and the county magistrate? The cadres being examined, as long as they were not criminals, were able to continue with their work. Their problems could be solved later. The officers without any problems were able to resume their official work.

All the rebel leaders of the leading groups of the county and municipal levels, educated youth and 'people's representatives' were permitted to resume their former work except where the provincial party committee confirmed that some individual cadres should not resume their former leading positions.

Due to a shortfall of talent in Anhui, Anhui province decided to call on cadres of Anhui origin to come back and join their hometown construction with favourable conditions as suggested by Comrade Gu Zhuoxin.

Under the direction of such special policies, the leading cadres of the provincial, prefectural and county levels were re-established fairly quickly.

The *People's Daily* published a long report entitled *Anhui is Catching Up* introducing the huge changes in Anhui's situation in prominent front-page headlines on 16 January 1978.

Affirmations from Deng Xiaoping and the *People's Daily*

Chapter 22

'Six Articles' Prelude to Rural Reform

In July 1977, one month after Wan Li came to govern Anhui, he saw an investigation report entitled: *Investigation of the Implementation of the Party's Rural Economic Policies and Views on Future Development* conducted by the CPC Chuxian county prefectural committee.

Actually the report had been written earlier. In the first six months of 1977, Wang Yuzhao, secretary of the CPC Chuxian county (Anhui province) prefectural committee, organised more than 300 cadres to carry out investigations among more than 400 production teams and wrote *Investigation of the Implementation of the Party's Rural Economic Policies and Views on Future Development* for the provincial party committee. In May, the CPC Chuxian county prefectural committee held a meeting to report the investigation in Dingyuan county and Wang Yuzhao invited the former first secretary of the provincial party committee to give a speech on the implementation of rural economic policies. The former first secretary said that there was absolutely no need to implement the specific policy and that making the greatest endeavours and strides would be the most effective policy. Since he was against the rural economic policy, Wang Yuzhao could not present the report at the meeting.

After Comrade Wan Li came to administer the work in Anhui, Wang Yuzhao officially submitted the report to the provincial party committee. Seeing that report, Wan Li highly valued it and immediately forwarded it to all the prefectural and municipal party committees. He pointed out: "It is a good beginning that resources in Chuxian county were organised to go deep among the people and carefully investigate rural economic policy. That issue merits attention in all quarters. The proposals in the report can serve as references for all locations." It was the first report Wan Li approved and forwarded when he came to administer Anhui.

Wang Yuzhao reporting on work to Wan Li, secretary of the CPC Anhui provincial committee

The rural problems of Anhui were prominently reflected during revelations, criticism and examination. Via Wang Guangyu, deputy secretary of the provincial party committee, Wan Li notified Zhou Yueli, secretary of Zeng Xisheng, director of the policy research office of the Anhui Provincial Agriculture Committee and the former first secretary of the provincial party committee to prepare to systematically report the rural information.

On 21 August, Zhou Yueli made a report in the Xiyuan meeting room at Daoxiang mansion. Comrades Zhao Shouyi and Wang Guangyu listened to the report. They discussed the realities of the countryside in Anhui.

Anhui used to be a rural area severely afflicted by 'leftist' policy and its rural economy was on the verge of collapse. During the 10 years of the 'cultural revolution', the total grain output languished at 10 million tonnes, the per capita annual income of farmers was about Rmb60 and the real living standard of farmers dropped by 30% due to price factors. According to estimates at that time, the per capita annual cost of living of farmers was about Rmb100. Therefore, up to 90% of production teams throughout the province did not have enough food and clothing, and farmers had little enthusiasm for production. There was a saying in the rural area that: "Farmers do not move to plough at the first whistle blast for production, they crane their necks to look at the second, hobble along at the third, remember at the edge of the field they forgot to bring hoes and return home to fetch them." What hope was there for the future of Anhui's rural areas under such slack work conditions?

Poverty forces farmers in Fengyang county to dig up edible wild herbs to allay their hunger

Zhou Yueli also systematically introduced the entire process and the gigantic effects of fixing farm output quotas for each household implemented by Zeng Xisheng, the first secretary of the CPC Anhui provincial committee in 1962. Talking continuously for more than five hours from 2pm until it got dark, he was still burning for more.

Wan Li said right away: "Food is the paramount necessity of the people. I would choose to have food to eat if I had to make a choice between a doctrine and the demand for food." He asked Zhou Yueli to take pertinent measures for a trial.

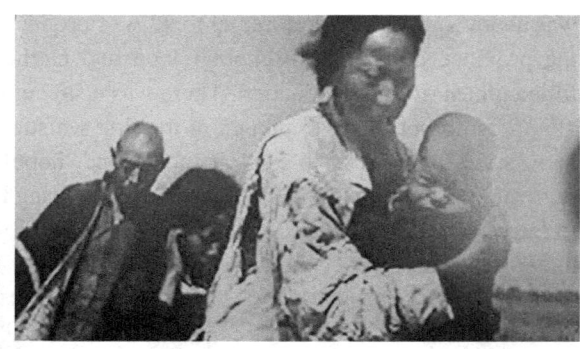

There was a serious exodus of people from Fengyang county

Zhou Yueli was fairly excited, organised 14 people at once to make an investigation for two months, classified the materials concerned and presented them to Wan Li.

Wan Li headed for Fengyang on 4 October for the first time. The CPC Shanghai municipal committee phoned to ask the CPC Anhui provincial committee to have the 'unemployed migrant people' taken back from Shanghai asylums. The 'unemployed migrant people' from Anhui accounted for 90% of the total, numbering 1,078, more than 600 from Fengyang county. He inspected some rural families in person and saw with his own eyes scenes of farmers scrambling onto slow-moving trains to get away.

With a heavy heart, Wan Li said: "Begging is an objective fact because of hunger resulting from failures in production. We must clarify the reasons for the production failures."

In early October, Wan Li gave instructions for a workshop to be held to implement rural policy in Chuxian county. By putting their heads together, the *Regulations on Problems Concerning the Present Rural Economic Policy (Draft)* were formulated. After that, two workshops were held for discussion and further modification. From 15 to 22 November 1977, Wan Li held a 'meeting of cadres at three levels' for cadres above the county level to discuss the Draft priorities. On 28 November, the *Regulations of the CPC Anhui Provincial Committee on the Problems Concerning Present Rural Economic Policy* (abbreviated to the 'six articles') was submitted to and approved by the standing committee of the CPC Anhui provincial committee.

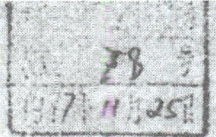

In November 1977, the CPC Anhui provincial committee formulated and issued the *Regulations on Problems Concerning Present Rural Economic Policy*

The main contents of the 'six articles' included: to properly operate and manage well the people's communes and positively develop socialist planned agriculture; to alleviate the burden of production teams and commune members; to honour the distribution and give consideration to the interests of the state, the collective and the individual; to allow and encourage commune members to run sideline businesses in their households and to sell their products in the market; to allow production teams to implement the responsibility system and to allocate responsibility for the farm work that could be finished by individuals to specific people. The core idea of the 'six articles' was to stress protection of and respect for the autonomous rights of production teams and to adjust measures to develop local production. The provincial party committee demanded that party committees at all levels take the implementation of the 'six articles' as a major priority.

Wan Li on an inspection tour in Anhui, October 1995

Wan Li said at a meeting: "The autonomous rights of production teams are a major rural problem at present. Stressing respect for the autonomous rights of production teams is to be against arbitrary and impractical decisions which have a huge impact on agricultural production! I think production will rise by more than 10% as long as we respect autonomous rights and get rid of arbitrary and impractical decisions. Respect for the autonomous rights of production teams includes: production autonomy; distribution autonomy; and labour force allocation autonomy. Production teams, as the basic accounting units, should have the right to decide what they plant and produce. But actually it is the higher authorities that make decisions regarding production and grain rations. Is there any enthusiasm left in that case? The essence of autonomous rights is that the producers are the real masters."

When the 'six articles' were passed, there was a flurry of activity. Gu Zhuoxin and Zhao Shouyi did not leave. Maybe they realised they would have to deal with the challenges of this 'snowstorm'. Zhao Shouyi, who was fond of playing jokes, held Wan Li's hand and said: "If you are put in jail, Zhuoxin and I will send food for you."

Wan Li responded: "How nice of you! It's worthwhile to be kept in jail for three years."

The regulations comprising the 'six articles' constituted a significant breakthrough in those years. It can be said that it was the first innovative document on rural economic policy adjustment in China after the 'gang of four' was smashed. It took the lead in breaking through the boundaries of the rigid 'leftist' rural policies and loosened the fetters on the farmers. It was warmly received by people when it came into force.

A correspondent concerned described the scenes as people fervently welcomed the 'six articles':

On an evening in mid-December, a production brigade in Sanshilipu commune, Liu'an county held a mass meeting to propagate the 'six articles'. People swarmed to the square and the people, old and young, male and female, listened to the document as if they were attending the theatre. On the platform, the cadres held the document and read it one word after another; under the stage, the people listened carefully in silence. The moment the reading was finished, some people under the stage shouted: "Once again!" When it came to key points to the liking of the people, such as allowing and encouraging commune members to operate private plots and household sideline production, the people under the stage shouted loudly: "Please repeat it!" "Read it slowly!" It was winter then. Someone asked an old man nearby: "Are you feeling cold?" He answered smilingly: "No, I'm not cold at all! Hearing about these new policies, I feel warm in my heart despite the cold weather. Even if it gets colder, it doesn't matter!."

The news about Anhui reported in the *People's Daily* expedited the implementation of national rural economic policy

The *People's Daily* and the Xinhua News Agency immediately reported about it. The *People's Daily* published a news report entitled: *The Birth of a Provincial Party Committee's Document* conspicuously on the front page on 3 February 1978.

Deng Xiaoping, vice chairman of the CPC central committee, who had recently resumed work, highly praised the 'six articles'. When he embarked on a foreign trip via Chengdu in the spring of 1978, he told the leaders in charge of Sichuan: you should liberate your minds regarding rural policy. You can refer to Wan Li's 'six articles' in Anhui. He also gave a copy of the 'six articles' to the leaders in charge of Sichuan in person. Soon afterwards, the CPC Sichuan provincial committee sent someone to Anhui to obtain the information, braved the 'leftist' pressure and promulgated the '12 articles' to revive and develop the rural economy in Sichuan.

Deng Xiaoping said in a later speech during an inspection tour in the south: China's reform started in the rural areas of Anhui. Wan Li made considerable contributions to it.

When Comrade Deng Xiaoping received Columbian Minister of Foreign Affairs Carlos Lemos Symonds on 1 October 1981, he said: "A female American professor visited Fengyang, historically the poorest place in China, and was deeply impressed... In the last two years things there have changed. The new agricultural policy, namely, the responsibility system, has been adopted and the farmers' enthusiasm has been aroused. It's still the same place but now t has changed for the better. It has turned over a new leaf in the past year or two and completely shaken off its poor and backward demeanour"

Chapter 23

Low-Profile, Large-Scale Rural Investigation

Wan Li grew up in the countryside, fought as a guerrilla in the Hebei-Shandong-Henan area in the anti-Japanese war, had day-to-day contact with farmers and had deep feelings for them. But after the liberation of China, he had been in charge of industry and construction and was no longer involved with rural work. The rural problem was very serious in Anhui and the farmers there lived a difficult life. Wan Li was unfamiliar with rural work. So he decided to spend three or four months inspecting the major rural areas in Anhui. In early November, 10 days before the 'six articles' were passed, he came to the old revolutionary base in Jinzhai county.

Wan Li inspects the rural area of Anhui

Wan Li went to inspect there without a big entourage, usually with two or three attendants in a car without prior notice. They were able to stop and start anytime, anywhere and went directly to villages and households. Wan Li thought that only in that way could he get to know the real situation. If he came across any problems, he consulted with the prefectural or county party committee concerned to solve it.

Jinzhai county was a famous 'county of generals' and one of the origins of the Fourth Red Army. During the war, 100,000 people sacrificed their lives there. In the 1950s, to effect a radical cure of the Huaihe river, two big international-standard reservoirs were built and 100,000 mu of fertile farmland was inundated. The hinterland of Dabie mountain suffered from two such cases in history. Additionally, the extreme 'leftist' line was prevalent there and it was much poorer than Wan Li could have imagined.

In a farmer's house, Wan Li's delegation met with an old man with two little girls about 10 years old on heaps of straw. The production team leader introduced the old man to Wan Li, and explained that the provincial party committee secretary had come to see him. At that, the old man abruptly stood up stark naked. Wan Li thought it was strange and asked why the two little girls were at home. The production team leader said they did not have trousers to wear.

Seeing veteran soldiers and family members of martyred soldiers living an impoverished and desolate life, Wan Li felt great grief and shed tears of sorrow. Wan Li said: "In those years they and their family members risked their lives and made great sacrifices and contributions to the revolution. We would not have been able to have our own country or our present happy life without them. But some of them do not have enough food to eat or enough clothes to wear now. How can we face them? We have a twinge of conscience!"

Wan Li immediately decided to appropriate a relief fund of Rmb1.2 million, 72.5 tonnes of cotton, 360,000 metres of cotton cloth and 250 tonnes of grain for the impoverished households in the old revolutionary base area in Jinzhai county. Wan Li also asked the county party committee to organise the compilation of the history of the Chinese revolutionary struggle and to build a revolutionary memorial museum for education in the revolutionary traditions.

In the winter of 1977, Wan Li's delegation of four came to southern Anhui. In Wuhu, they were told that Wuhu, historically reputed to be one of China's four major rice markets, was no longer what it used to be after grain was purchased and marketed by the state in a unified way. A farmer in Yunling said: "We were even able to offer food to tens of thousands of soldiers in wartime. Generally speaking there was no problem to have enough food then. But our present living standard is unexpectedly inferior to what it was in those years."

Wan Li with students of the youth class of the University of Science and Technology of China in Anhui in 1978

After numerous inspections on his tour of southern Anhui, Wan Li came to the old disaster area in the countryside around Fuyang. It was the 23rd day of the 12th lunar month. Wan Li visited each household in a village north of Taihe city and asked how they had prepared for the new year. He found that some peasant households did not have flour and were worried whether they could eat dumplings to celebrate the new year. Wan Li said sadly: "My hometown in Dongping is not far from here. Even the poorest family would try every means to eat dumplings when new year comes even in the old society. You see, destitute Yang Bailao in the movie *The White-Haired Girl* would rack his brains to eat dumplings and 'buy red thread' to bind his daughter's plaits. How terrible it would be if people could not have dumplings to eat to celebrate the spring festival?"

Wan Li visiting the countryside in Anhui

He promptly instructed the department concerned to try whatever they could to dispense 1.5kg of wheat to each farmer so that every household could have dumplings to eat.

Walking out of the village house of a farmer surnamed Zhang from Feidong county to Dingyuan county in late January 1978, Wan Li said anxiously: "I only heard that it was poor in the past but I didn't expect it was that poor. You see, all his belongings were not worth Rmb30 and could be taken away simply with a stick."

In the spring of 1978, Wan Li's delegation came from Dingyuan county to the county town of Luqiao and saw a young farmer resting on a bank beside the road. It was already late March, sunny and warm. But the farmer still wore worn-out cotton-padded clothes. Wan Li walked up and talked about daily life with him. Then the people did not watch TV and did not know Wan Li. They talked freely with nobody else around.

After talking about production and life, Wan Li asked whether he needed anything. He undid his winter jacket collar and patted his belly: "I need nothing more than to have enough food to eat!" Wan Li asked whether he had other needs besides that modest demand. The farmer smiled and said: "Fewer dried sweet potatoes!" After that, Wan Li said: "You see, how good our farmers are! Their requirements are not high, but the lowest. However, we still cannot meet their needs 28 years after liberation!"

Wan Li chatting with farmers to familiarise himself with the situation

Wan Li conducting a grassroots investigation

During his four-month large-scale rural investigation, Wan Li directly experienced and thoroughly familiarised himself with the situation of the poor rural areas of Anhui. At a plenary session of the provincial party committee in early 1978, he primarily proposed "to concentrate on production and do a good job of agricultural production" explicitly throughout the province. At a workshop for the county party committee secretaries in the poor areas, Wan Li said with emotion: "As long as production is well managed, you can stipulate whatever policy demands you like." He stood up, tapped his hand on the table and said emotionally in a loud voice: "As I said last time, if I find any beggars in any county after autumn this year, I will take them to beg at the door of the county party committee secretary! What is socialism in the presence of beggars? What's the superiority of socialism if farmers are still so poor 30 years or more after liberation?"

Chapter 24

Restoring Order Out of Chaos in Early Rural Policy

Anhui's 'six articles' were formulated and issued during a wave of activity when the whole nation was learning from Dazhai and making the transition through poverty to socialism.

At about the same time that Wan Li issued the 'six articles' in the winter of 1977, the central committee issued document no. 49 and proposed changing 10% of the production teams to be production brigades comprising the basic accounting unit in the winter of 1977 and spring of 1978.

The contents of the 'six articles' were totally inconsistent with those in the 'learn from Dazhai' campaign and the central committee's document no. 49. In recalling that part of history, Wan Li said: "Especially, the autonomous rights of production teams was a major problem in rural work during those years. Stressing respect for the autonomous rights of production teams was to oppose arbitrary and impractical decisions. That problem had a big impact on agricultural production. That point was only mentioned in the 'six articles' on operation and management. Later I found it to be very important and suggested documenting it separately."

"The higher authorities were able to decide what and how the production teams planted as the basic accounting unit, and even the products and grain ration. How could this motivate the farmers' enthusiasm? I felt that the people's communes actually enslaved the farmers, deprived them of their autonomous production rights and of their right to dispose of their possessions, and tremendously depressed the farmers' enthusiasm. I sensed that problem but could not point it out then because the system of people's communes was protected by the constitution."

In early 1978, the CPC central committee decided to hold a national on-site meeting to 'popularise the experiences of Dazhai county' with the attendance of the first provincial party committee secretaries of all provinces. Wan Li thought: "Agricultural productivity depends mainly on manual tools and the farmers' hands directed by their minds. If the farmers are confused and lack enthusiasm, how can the hands work diligently? How can production be improved? We should not follow the national practice implemented in other places nationwide. But it cannot be pointed out at the meeting and it will be useless even if it is mentioned there. How to deal with it? According to the notice, the first provincial party committee secretary should attend the conference. But I found an excuse not to go. I let Secretary Zhao Shouyi attend on my behalf. I asked him only to listen and look but not to say anything. Anhui's farmers do not support the practice of Dazhai. We cannot learn from it and we cannot afford to learn from it. Definitely, we cannot oppose it in public. I asked him not to say anything or convey the contents of the meeting. In brief, we must be responsible for the people of the province, do whatever we can within our power and persistently adhere to and implement the 'six articles'."

Dazhai production brigade in Xiyang county

During the big debate on practice being the sole criterion to test truth in April, Wan Li aired his view: "In accordance with Anhui's realities, the present problem is primarily how to mobilise the farmers' enthusiasm rather than the problem of mechanisation. It is the most important policy issue. Without farmers' enthusiasm, there is nothing. The commune system characterised by 'being large in size and collective in nature', 'rigidly managed transition' and 'general distinction of work points according to different criteria' not only fails to mobilise farmers' enthusiasm but, on the contrary, dampens and depresses their enthusiasm. To fully mobilise their enthusiasm, efforts should be made to bring them economic benefits and guarantee their political and democratic rights. Therefore, we should lay special emphasis on respecting the autonomous rights of the production team."

The 'six articles' won people's applause but also aroused the dissatisfaction and objection of some leaders of the central committee in charge of agriculture. Some people believed Anhui province was applying 'capitalism' and adopting a wrong line; others believed that Anhui province was implementing rural economic policy to 'give petty favours without handling the crux of the problem' and that it was mobilising the enthusiasm of capitalists at the expense of Chairman Mao's revolutionary line. Consequently, they organised some people to specifically criticise the practice of Anhui province, but not by name.

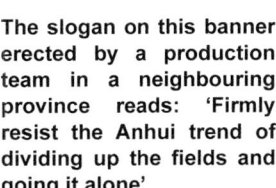

The slogan on this banner erected by a production team in a neighbouring province reads: 'Firmly resist the Anhui trend of dividing up the fields and going it alone'

On 13 May 1978, the *People's Daily* published a signed article of more than 6,000 words by 'the joint report group stationed in Dazhai' entitled: *Good Experiences of Xiyang County in Mobilising Farmers' Socialist Enthusiasm*. The article stated: "People at Dazhai never talk about mobilising enthusiasm in the general sense but socialist enthusiasm. People at Dazhai bear in mind the basic line of the party. They believe that 'socialism will not move ahead if capitalism is not eliminated'. The unhealthy trend of capitalism is seductive to some ideologically backward farmers and deals a heavy blow to honest farmers who really advocate socialism; if the leaders' attitude is ambiguous, the people will be in ideological chaos, the unhealthy trend of capitalism will become increasingly serious and the socialist economy will be destroyed."

Any reasonably intelligent person realised that this was targeted at Anhui.

Aware of the situation, Wan Li did not waver in the slightest. He said: "Views on Anhui's practice differ. Some say we are 'rightists' applying 'capitalism' while others agree with us but don't dare to air their agreement in public. We will continue to do what we need to do, no matter what others say. People will surely draw their own conclusions. So will history! We cannot learn from brigade accounting, 'rigidly managed transition' and 'general distinction of work points according to different criteria'. Can we be forced to learn? They can give up their private plots, refuse to allow commune members to raise pigs and cancel market trade. But it won't do in Anhui."

Wan Li added: "Since the leaders talked about it in the *People's Daily*, we can also write articles to refute them. They criticised us not by name. We can also criticise them not by name accordingly. We can convince people by reasoning with facts."

His views were implemented. On 21 January 1979, the Xinhua News Agency published an article entitled: *Achieving High Yields in a Year of Disasters and Great Change - An Investigative Report on Contracting Production to the Group Implemented by the Weiying Production Team of Lai'an County in Anhui Province*. The investigative report of more than 6,000 characters thoroughly introduced and fully affirmed the specific practice and experiences of production contracted to each production group. It was the first time that 'contracting production to the group' was published in a public newspaper.

The correspondent's series of reports on Anhui's rural reform from January through March thoroughly introduced the practice of Anhui to promote the household contract responsibility system, affirmed the experiences of Anhui and undoubtedly advanced nationwide rural reform.

Looking at rural reform in retrospect, Wan Li said on 10 October 1997: "If Dazhai's practice of 'taking class struggle as the guideline' and 'rigidly managed transition' had not been avoided, the cause of concentrating on production could not have been promoted and persisted in. It was actually the first and the most important measure in restoring order out of chaos."

Wan Li profoundly analysed Dazhai's problems: "Dazhai was originally a good example, especially of self-reliance, hard work and plain living, which should be carefully studied and carried forward. Nevertheless, during the 'cultural revolution', Mao Zedong called on the nation to learn from Dazhai as a good example. Therefore, things went in the opposite direction. However, China has a large expanse of land and the conditions of different rural areas differ sharply. It is in itself unscientific, impractical and unrealistic to learn from Dazhai simply and exclusively. Moreover, learning from Dazhai then was not about learning how to improve agricultural production or construction in mountainous areas but how to intensify class struggle and how to facilitate the transition to socialism by means of 'large-scale criticism of revisionism and capitalism'. Dazhai also indulged in self-aggrandisement, regarded itself as right on all issues, blatantly aggravated 'leftist' mistakes and was reduced to being a tool of the 'gang of four' to promote the 'leftist' line."

Chapter 25

Biggest Drought in 100 Years Induces 'Lending Land to Survive Famine'

Signs of drought had just started to appear during the summer harvest of 1978, the first bumper harvest season Wan Li saw after the 'six articles' were formulated. During the dragon boat festival, Wan Li went directly to a dozen wheat-threshing sites in five counties including Changfeng county and talked openly with farmers harvesting the wheat. He saw that the threshing was almost finished and witnessed the happy scene of a bumper harvest. The summer harvest was on course to rise by 10%.

Faced with people's general anxiety about high grain requisitions, Wan Li and other provincial party committee leaders unanimously agreed to change the past practice of failing to consider reality and blindly requisitioning as much food as possible. The provincial party committee decided not to requisition food from production teams that collectively allocated grain rations of less than 37.5kg to commune members during the two months from allocation of the summer harvest to the autumn harvest.

Wan Li said: "How to properly treat farmers is a key issue."

The farmers waited for the rain to plant in autumn after the wheat harvest. It was a year that witnessed the biggest, longest, most serious drought since the founding of the PRC. It did not rain in most areas throughout the province for eight or nine months continuously, resulting in the lowest annual rainfall since 1949. The main course of the Huaihe river experienced drought for 10 months in a row from June to April the next year. The five major reservoirs of the Pishihang watershed were empty by late June. Some medium-sized and small reservoirs, dams and rivers were basically dried up. Most areas had difficulty finding water to counter the drought. Throughout the province, 1.61 million hectares of summer crops

Biggest Drought in 100 Years Induces 'Lending Land to Survive Famine'

and 2.78 million hectares of autumn crops suffered drought, accounting for 64% of the agricultural acreage.

The prolonged drought crippled the autumn harvest and planting in many places. Based on in-depth investigation and research, the provincial party committee held an emergency meeting on 1 September.

Wan Li said: "Anhui's agriculture has inevitably failed this year. No one can do much about it. The grain harvest of the entire province was millions of tonnes less than planned while 45 million people have to have three meals a day. It fully demonstrates the severity of the problem." "It is critical to mobilise everyone's enthusiasm. Otherwise, the wheat will not be planted even if we never sleep."

Gu Zhuoxin (first from right) and Wang Yuzhao (second from right) seek information about the drought

Secretary Zhao Shouyi's speech greatly inspired Wan Li. He said: "The other day when I was in Huaibei, an old farmer told me it suffered from a severe drought in 1960 when Zeng Xisheng implemented the field responsibility (or responsible field) system. The drought then was similar to the one this year. Farmers practicing the household contract responsibility system all planted wheat but after rushing headlong into mass action they could not plant the wheat, resulting in people starving to death the next year.

Wan Li (left) in discussion with Zhao Shouyi to learn about the situation in 1978

Wan Li nodded and said: "Autumn planting is crucial for this winter and next spring. We should not waste large tracts of rural land. Otherwise, people's lives will be more difficult next year. We should plan ahead. We'd rather divide up some cultivated land among the farmers, give full scope to their potential and plant as much 'subsistence wheat' as possible to tide us over the drought disaster rather than be exposed to waste."

Zhao Shouyi responded: "This is called believing in the masses, depending on the masses and lending land to survive famine."

Wan Li asked everyone present to air their views on the idea of 'lending land to survive famine', which aroused heated debate at the meeting.

Some people said: we say that the big drought calls for big actions, that lending land to survive famine is a practice akin to not believing in the superiority of the collective economy and that enthusiasm mobilised in that way is not socialist enthusiasm. Others asked: Why is the land lent to individuals of the commune rather than the collective? It is actually dividing up the fields and going it alone to plant under the pretext of 'lending land to survive famine'. It is a problem of orientation and line.

Wan Li answered calmly: "The land we will lend is 'land that cannot be planted by the collective'. If the collective can plant it, there will be no such problem. It is a general principle that it is better for either the collective or the individual to plant wheat and vegetables than to leave it in drought. The grain planted by either the collective or individuals can satisfy hunger and help us tide over the disaster. In the extraordinary period of serious drought, we must break with convention and adopt special policies to pull through the drought."

With a sigh, Wan Li uttered: "We have no other way out except to use such an expedient."

But then he said quickly, revealing his feelings: "Let's put the problem of line and direction aside. Aren't we ashamed to shout about serving the people when farmers don't have enough food to eat even 30 years after the founding of the PRC? How does that prove the superiority of socialism? With an empty stomach?"

The meeting lasted late into the night. The provincial party committee decided to 'lend land to survive famine': any land that could not be cultivated by the collective was able to be lent to commune members to plant wheat or vegetables; farmers were encouraged to reclaim as much wasteland as possible; whoever planted could harvest and own the crops, and the state did not requisition grain for planned distribution or assign farmers the task of requisitioning.

After the meeting, Gu Zhuoxin reminded Wan Li: "Dear Wan, I'm not against 'lending land to survive famine'. However, you know, the debate on the 'six articles' has not yet run its course nationwide. Aren't you afraid that history may repeat itself if land is lent to tide people over their difficulties?"

Wan Li responded: "It's not a big deal. We cannot satisfy the higher authorities and the grassroots people at the same time. The farmers are our grassroots brothers and I've no other choice but to let them have enough food to eat. I'll be satisfied if they do not denounce me! What's more, the worst that can happen is that I may be toppled once again!"

The decision to 'lend land to survive drought' was warmly welcomed by farmers. Farmers throughout the province, male and female, old and young, joined in farming for 20 days and overfulfilled the task of autumn planting by more than 3.3million hectares which seemed impossible. Most of the land edge was planted with oil-seed rape, broad beans and wheat. According to estimates, the measure of 'lending land to plant wheat' alone enabled the area for autumn planting to rise by more than 670,000 hectares provincewide.

Wan Li heads an Anhui delegation to the US in September 1979; the picture shows Wan Li and his wife Bian Tao greeting American onlookers

Chapter 26

Shannan District, Feixi County Contracts Production to Households

About five million people starved to death in Anhui during the three years of natural disasters and the trend of exaggerating production figures in the 1960s. Zeng Xisheng, the first provincial party committee secretary made key contributions to China's revolution and had deep feelings for the farmers. After much introspection and atonement, he implemented the 'responsibility field' system throughout the province of Anhui in 1961. The specific practice was to: contract production to the team, fix production quotas for the field, determine work points for production, contract farm work to each household and calculate rewards and compensation in proportion to the amount of work done.

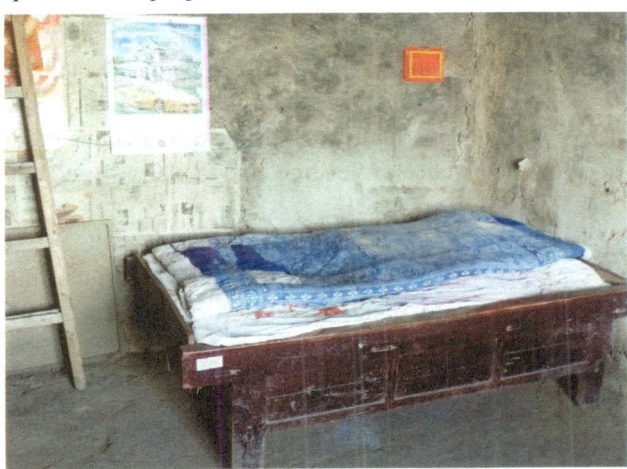

A worn-out bed and mattress used by the farmers of Xiaojing village, Feixi county during the three years of disasters in the 1960s

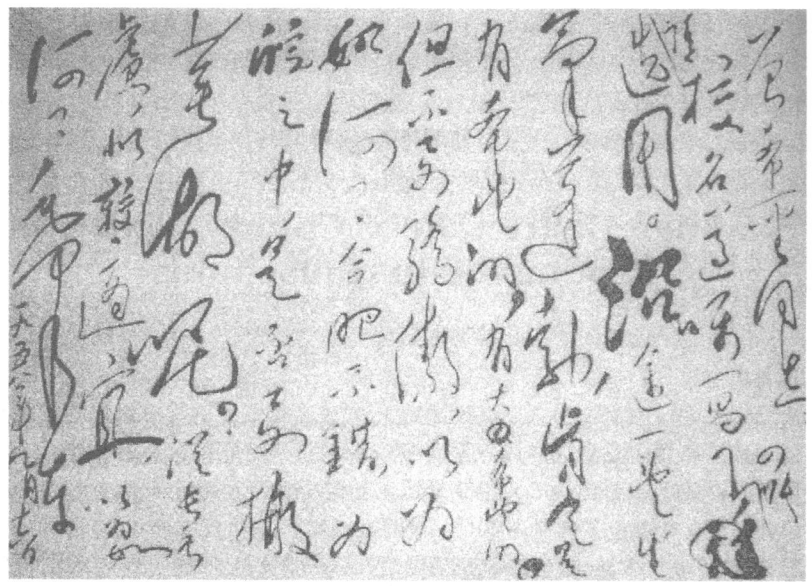

A letter written by Mao Zedong to Zeng Xisheng on 16 September 1958

The 'responsibility field' system was implemented in Anhui for only one year but was stopped because Zeng Xisheng was removed from office and criticised. But Anhui's agriculture that year obtained a bumper harvest and the food problem of the farmers was solved immediately and effectively. Anhui's farmers generally benefited from the 'responsibility field' system and took or created the opportunity to implement contracting production to each household. The practice of 'lending land to plant wheat' could not be stopped once it had been applied.

On 15 September 1978, Chang Zhenying, the CPC Feixi county committee secretary, rushed to inspect the work of autumn planting in Shannan district. Tang Maolin, the CPC Shannan district committee secretary, reported that: "The provincial party committee's decision to lend land to survive famine was good. But the practice of lending 30% of the land was less effective. The problema could have been solved by lending all the land and contracting production to each household like Zeng Xisheng did in 1961."

After a long silence, Chang Zhenying finally said: "It's better to lend the

Shannan District, Feixi County Contracts Production to Households

land rather than divide it up. You can stay in Huanghua production brigade and make experiments in Huanghua."

In the Huanghua Oil Plant on the night of reporting to Chang Zhenying, Tang Maolin held a general membership meeting of the party branch. Among the 24 party members of the production brigade, 23 attended it. At the meeting, Tang Maolin primarily led the rest to study the 'six articles' and the decision to 'lend land to plant wheat for survival' and called on others to pool their wisdom and efforts. The attendees unanimously reflected that it was a good method to lend the land but 30% was not enough; besides, the land was 'lent' and the commune members were worried it would be taken back. They did not rest assured.

"We can definitely follow the responsibility field system and contract production to each household." After a heated debate, the attendees concluded 'four fixes and one reward' at dawn.

This meant: 1) Fixing the land - one mu (0.0667 hectares) of land was contracted to each person of the whole production brigade to plant wheat and half a mu to plant oilseed rape; 2) Fixing the cost of production - the production team gave the farmers subsidies of Rmb5 per mu to buy seeds and fertiliser; 3) Fixing the output - farmers were obliged to turn over 100kg of wheat per mu and 50kg of rape per mu to the production team; 4) Fixing the work points: 200 work points were recorded per mu. In terms of rewards and punishment, overproduction was rewarded and for underproduction the shortfall had to be compensated for.

Due to the lessons drawn from the mistakes in 1961, production brigade director Xie Qifu said: "It should be renamed rather than being called the responsibility field system." Tang Maolin said: "We should make two kinds of preparation. It is contracting for the people but lending to the outside." On the morning of 16 September 1978, Huanghua production brigade held a cadre meeting, announced its decision and had a general meeting of commune members in the afternoon. The commune members applauded the decision until their hands turned red. The moment the meeting ended, the whole production brigade took prompt action. In less than two days, 1,420 mu of the 1,700 mu of land belonging to the whole production brigade was subcontracted to each household.

A monument to the agricultural production responsibility system erected at the end of Xiaojing village, Feixi county

Shannan District, Feixi County Contracts Production to Households

On the evening of 15 September 1978, Huanghua production brigade of Shishu commune, Shannan district, Feixi county held a general meeting of branch members and decided to contract production to each household. The daring feat raised the magnificent curtain for China's agricultural reform

Before daybreak when the policy began to be implemented, some farmers of the Huanghua production brigade got up early while it was still dark, and worked in their own responsibility fields by lamplight, digging, ploughing and pounding the hard, arid turf which buffalos could not plough with shovels, rakes and mallets. Only on the first day, the Huanghua production brigade planted more than 40 mu of wheat and rape.

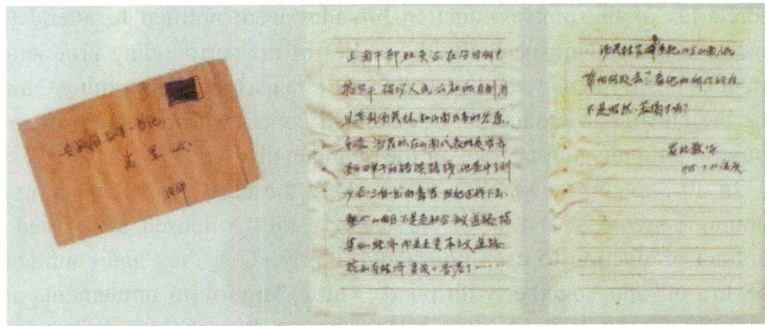

Resistance from all sides did not sway the minds of Xiaojing village farmers from contracting production to each household in the least but, on the contrary, strengthened their confidence in perservering with it

On 21 May 1979, Wan Li held the first agricultural workshop on contracting production to each household in Xiaojing village, Feixi county, Anhui province. Pictured are bronze statues erected in front of the former site to commemorate the workshop (second from left is Wan Li)

The Shannan district party committee held an on-site meeting at the Huanghua production brigade. Originally only secretaries of the party committees of the Shannan, Shishu and Fanghu communes and branch secretaries of the nine production brigades were notified to attend the on-site meeting. Unexpectedly, the cadres of the surrounding production brigades heard the news and rushed to the site early in the morning. News that the Huanghua production brigade had contracted production to each household rapidly spread all over the Shannan district.

On 20 September, Xiaojing village held the third general meeting of commune members and all of the heads of the 25 households agreed to contract production to each household. Fairly soon, they had contracted 158 mu of land, together with ponds, cattle, large farm implements and seeds of the whole production brigade to the households; furthermore, they cancelled the 'four fixes and one reward', the mode of distribution documented by the Huanghua production brigade, and stipulated that farmers could keep the harvest for themselves except for the part turned over. All these efforts and measures further improved and facilitated the household contract responsibility system of production.

Tang Maolin held four meetings in five days and the Huanghua production brigade's experiences immediately spread to the entire Shannan district. Some 77% of the 1,006 production teams of the 78 production brigades of the seven communes of the whole district implemented the household contract responsibility system for production and rapidly aroused great mass fervour for resisting drought and rush-planting. By 10 November, a total of 5,333 hectares of wheat and 1,333 hectares of barley had been planted, more than twice the area planted in normal years and the quality of autumn planting was also significantly better than in past years.

Chapter 27

Chuxian Prefecture's Three 'Secret Weapons'

The CPC Chuxian county prefectural committee held a four-level cadre meeting for the whole district in September 1978 to make arrangements for production, self-help, and autumn ploughing and planting. At that time, the debate on 'practice being the sole criterion for testing truth' had been going on for months. With the implementation of the 'six articles' of the provincial party committee, the 'leftist' mistakes in the rural areas had begun to be rectified, the ideology of the cadres and the masses had been activated, and the old economic institutions in eastern Anhui had been impacted.

During the group discussion of the prefectural party committee meeting for cadres of four levels, many commune cadres asked the question: why on earth has our agriculture not developed over such a long period? There might be reasons why agriculture in one or two individual communes has not developed. But what's the reason why 242 communes throughout the district have not developed? Is it because we are all fools?

The prefectural party committee secretary Wang Yuzhao asked all present to air their views freely and democratically. In the ensuing discussions, the practices of the Weiying production team of Lai'an county contracting production to the group, Xinjie commune of Tianchang county contracting production to labourers and the communes of Lai'an county promoting the cadre post responsibility system all attracted much attention at the meeting.

The Weiying production team of Yangdu production brigade of Yanchen commune in Lai'an county had implemented the 'three contracts and one reward' contract responsibility system. To overcome the malpractice of headlong mass action, as early as the spring of 1978, the production team of only 104 people from 21 households recounted their experience of 'three contracts' (contracting for labour, production and charges) and one reward (for exceeding the production quota), dividing up the team into two operation teams and implementing 'six fixes', namely, fixing the labour, land, output, work points, reward and punishment, and team leadership. In 1978, the summer grain harvest increased by up to 50% and the per capita income rose by 30%.

Wang Yuzhao in a round-table discussion with farmers to investigate the implementation of rural economic policy

The Xinjie commune in Tianchang county had contracted cotton production to each household. It was a cotton-planting area with low output and severe losses. The farmers there were not willing to plant cotton and the state plan could not be implemented. After the 'six articles' were implemented, the commune applied the 'six fixes, one reward and three unifies' responsibility system for the professional cotton-planting teams which entailed fixing the crew, output, remuneration, charges and management measures; giving rewards for overproduction and deducting work points for production shortfalls according to the specific situation based on the output per mu; unifying planned planting, technology management and use of farm cattle, farm tools, water and fertiliser. Although the drought was serious, nevertheless a good cotton harvest was assured and output rose from 14.5kg per mu in 1977 to more than 30kg per mu in 1978.

The grassroots cadre post responsibility system formulated by the communes in Lai'an county gave rewards or penalites at the end of the year according to the completion of the production targets for grain, oil, cotton, pigs, poultry and eggs for the whole year.

These measures were 'forbidden zones' in those years. They were applied secretly and were hence called 'secret weapons' with the higher authorities kept in the dark. However, they drastically mobilised farmers' enthusiasm and increased all-round production despite the drought.

Wang Yuzhao came to Hefei in November. Wan Li asked him to talk about information concerning the rural areas. Wang Yuzhao reported the prominent problems in the rural areas, drought relief and the role of the three 'secret weapons' to Wan Li in detail for up to three hours. Wan Li attached great importance to it and instructed him to make a detailed survey of the 'three models' and write a report for the provincial party committee.

After reviewing the three survey reports of the CPC Chuxian county committee, Wan Li immediately notified the local party committee about conducting experiments. To this end, the CPC Chuxian county committee issued document no. 96, circulated the three survey reports to the whole district and required all the counties to implement experiments. After the document was circulated, all the counties were required to expand the scope of their experiments and many communes and brigades competed to be among the experimental units. By late March 1979, 68.3% of all production teams in Chuxian county district were contracting production to the group

Three hours not only spanned the report of Wang Yuzhao but also much of the time was spent with a sincere exchange of views on rural policies. As the first leaders of the province and the prefecture, they both foresaw the irresistible historical tide of contracting production to each household. Nevertheless, how to break through the absolutely forbidden zones for the time being? How to deal with the conflicts between the realities and the spirit of the central committee's document?

Wan Li and Wang Yuzhao

Wan Li said openly what was on his mind: "Whether or not our policy facilitates the development of productivity depends on whether it can fully mobilise farmers' enthusiasm for production. It is the basic essence of the central committee's document."

"The central committee's policy is to manage the reality and also to proceed from reality. Reality is constantly changing and knowledge of reality is limited and needs a certain period of time. Therefore, any policy should be ceaselessly improved, enhanced and tested in practice. Policy itself is both serious and flexible. For this reason, the principle of correctly dealing with the party's policy and the instructions of the higher authorities is to proceed from reality and to seek truth from facts."

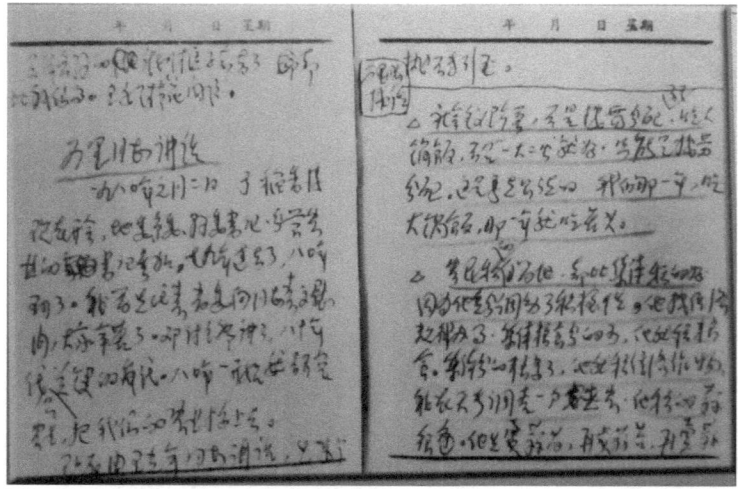

The minutes of Wan Li's speech recorded by prefectural party committee secretary Wang Yuzhao during a meeting on agriculture in Anhui province. Wan Li pointed out: "Socialism isn't egalitarianism. The management methods can be diverse but the core of the responsibility system is to mobilise people's enthusiasm and link the results of production closely with the individuals' interests"

"If some specific regulations clearly are not adapted to reality, it is a good test of a leader's policy level and ideological level to see whether they proceed from reality and seek truth from facts or apply the regulations mechanically."

"China features a large expanse of land, a large population, sharply different natural conditions and a complex situation. It is impractical and impossible to require each document or instruction of the central committee to be perfectly adapted to different areas nationwide and different situations. Indiscriminately copying everything without considering reality will inevitably be 'a sweeping approach' and will not generate good effects."

"The situations and the reasons concerned should be clarified if the measures are not adapted to the local situation or cannot be implemented. Proposals should be made and reported to the higher-level party organs. If the higher-level party organs do not agree with our ideas, we can reserve our view and unswervingly obey the decision of the higher-level party organs. That is our principle for dealing with such problems."

Chapter 28

Fengyang Implements 'All-Round Responsibility System' while Xiaogang Contracts Production to Households

Fengyang county lies in the northeast of Anhui, where historically crops failed nine years out of ten. Farmers lost their homes, fled famine and begged for a living. The famous Fengyang flower drum dance has been used by the destitute as a tool for begging. Backwardness and poverty were typical characteristics of Anhui.

The moment Wan Li arrived in Anhui, he took the county as the focus of his work. After the 'six articles' were transmitted to the lower levels in April 1978, the first county party committee secretary Chen Tingyuan immediately implemented three specific measures aligned with Fengyang's realities: private plots, (animal) feed land and fruit trees were taken back from commune members and returned to farmers; agricultural production was arranged according to local conditions following natural laws; more dry crops were planted and heads of corn were not sold.

Geomorphological image of the former Xiaogang village where crops failed nine years out of ten

Fengyang Implements 'All-Round Responsibility System' while Xiaogang Contracts Production to Households

Wan Li's speech at the sixth congress of the CPC Anhui military region entitled: 'Contracting Output to Households is a Type of Socialist Production Responsibility System' - 1 February 1979

Afterwards, the county party committee started from the year-end distribution and established the 'one group and four fixes' production responsibility system under the premise of 'ownership of three levels based on the production team': dividing up production among several work groups and fixing tasks, time, quality and work points for them. That practice was remarkably superior to the 'headlong mass action' in the 'cultural revolution' and was warmly welcomed by people.

After the 'one group and four fixes' system was promoted throughout the county, Zhan Shaozhou, secretary of Mahu commune in Fengyang, took the lead in implementing the production responsibility system featuring 'group work and calculating work according to production' and 'rewards related to production': group work, fixing production to groups, calculating work according to production, rewards for overproduction, compensation for underproduction, contracting the expenses and distributing what was saved to the groups.

On 28 April, Chen Tingyuan held an agricultural production meeting in Wudian district and Zhan Shaozhou gained Chen Tingyuan's support on the condition of avoiding publicity. However, Mahu commune's 'production responsibility system linked with remuneration' spread like wildfire and was successively implemented by the production teams of some communes in Fengyang.

On 18 July 1978, Wan Li came to inspect Fengyang and Chen Tingyuan reported to him the 'production responsibility system linked with remuneration'. Soon afterwards, Zhou Yueli from the Anhui Province Agriculture Committee and the investigation team dispatched by the rural policy research office of the central committee made a field investigation of Mahu commune and the 'production responsibility system linked with remuneration' won the affirmation and support of Wan Li.

There was a drought in Anhui in 1978 and the rainfall in Fengyang was less than 50% of what it was in ordinary years. Nonetheless, by implementing the 'production responsibility system linked with remuneration' Mahu commune produced a miracle in that eight out of ten of its production teams kept production level and the remaining two teams increased production.

Chen Tingyuan talks cordially with farmers about the 'production responsibility system linked with remuneration' approved and supported by Wan Li

Xiaogang village lies in the east of Fengyang county. The Xiaogang production team made about Rmb20 per capita and had grain rations of 50-100kg in 1978. The villagers had to eat grain supplied by the state for

Fengyang Implements 'All-Round Responsibility System' while Xiaogang Contracts Production to Households

five to eight months each year and even had to beg to survive. In the winter, Fengyang county promoted the 'group-based contract system' and the Xiaogang villagers were also very keen to divide up 20 households into four groups. Before long, conflicts occurred inside the groups. Therefore, each group was further 'divided' into two parts. There were in total eight subgroups. Each subgroup comprised only two or three households between father and son or between brothers. Nevertheless, they quarrelled a few days later and did not cooperate well.

A group photo of some leaders of the all-round responsibility system of Xiaogang village in front of their former residences

On the afternoon of 24 November, the production team held a meeting and the attendees agreed that they would starve the next year if things went on like that. They regarded fixing farm output quotas for each household as the best way to have enough food to eat without the need to flee from the famine or go out begging. Aware of the danger of that problem, the attendees decided to write a written pledge at the meeting and do it secretly. The production group leader Yan Hongjun asked deputy production group leader Yan Hongchang to take paper and pen. After writing, Yan Hongchang read it once again: Date: December 1978; Site: Yan Lihua's house; Contents: We hereby divide up the fields among each household and the household heads should sign or seal their names. Each household should guarantee all its members turn over the agricultural tax paid in grain and should not ask the state for money or grain; otherwise, we cadres will be willingly put into jail or killed and the commune members will guarantee to raise our children until they are 18 years old. Anybody who agrees should sign or seal their names.

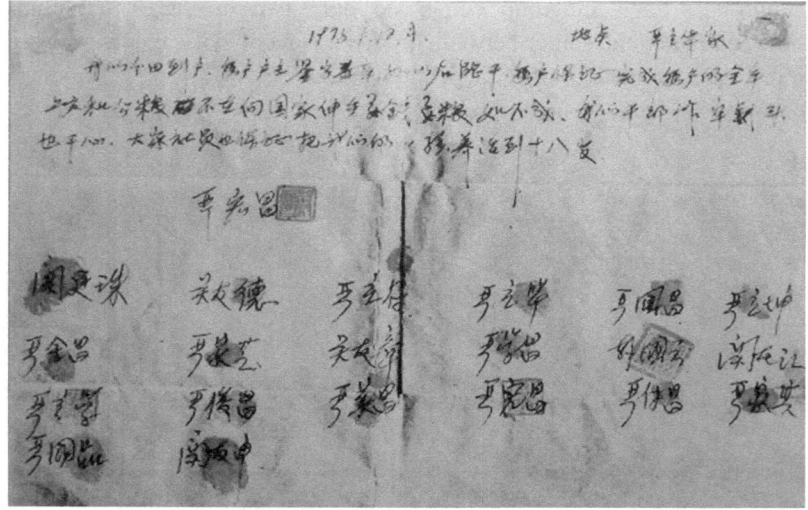

In February 1979, 18 villagers of Xiaogang village, Fengyang county took great risks to put their fingerprints on a contract for the 'household contract responsibility system'. It was the first responsibility contract nationwide

Yan Hongchang was the first to sign his name and put his fingerprint on the contract, followed by 18 members of farmers' households on the site at the risk of being killed or jailed.

Afterwards, they cast lots to allot domestic animals and farm implements and measured the land that very night, with everything done by the next morning.

Walls have ears. Even though the Xiaogang villagers did not leak any information, members of neighbouring communes could tell something was up because other teams worked in groups but only Xiaogang villagers worked by household. Upon learning that information, the commune cadres criticised the Xiaogang team at the cadre meeting: "Even if a team is small, consisting of only two or three households, it is still a collective.

Fengyang Implements 'All-Round Responsibility System' while Xiaogang Contracts Production to Households

But a household is different." They went on to announce: "If Xiaogang village does not join together with us, they will not get access to fertilisers, seeds or loans."

In November 1980, people of Fengyang county, Anhui province who were accustomed to eating resold grain requisitioned by the state for 26 years in a row achieved increases in the total output of grain and rapeseed oil plants of between 40% and 50% after the responsibility system was implemented compared with the output in 1977. Pictured are geese raised by the sideline team of Qijian production brigade of Chengnan commune

The Xiaogang production team leader passed on the commune's view but the commune members responded in unison not to be combined. They could figure out other methods of finance and use solid manure or borrow cattle or grass if they had no access to loans, fertilisers, cattle or grass.

On 10 April 1979, Chen Tingyuan came to Liyuan commune. Hearing that Xiaogang village had implemented a household contract responsibility system, he immediately came to Xiaogang village. Seeing all the families busy with production and the crops growing healthily, and hearing Yan Hongchang tell stories of hardship, Chen Tingyuan said to the commune cadres with all sincerity that: "They've been desperately poor. How can they engage in capitalism? At most, they will harvest more grain and solve the problem of survival. Let's wait and see how they get on a year from now."

Leaders of Xiaogang village, Fengyang county who implemented the 'all-round responsibility system' in those years, pictured in front of the village

Farmers of Fengyang county playing flower drums to celebrate the good harvest after farm output quotas had been fixed for each household

Fengyang Implements 'All-Round Responsibility System' while Xiaogang Contracts Production to Households

A sculpture of the 18 farmers of Fengyang county putting their fingerprints on the contract

On 25 April 2016, General Secretary Xi Jinping held a rural reform workshop in Xiaogang village, Fengyang county, Anhui province with the participation of local prefectural, municipal and county leaders, members of the 'two committees (branch party committee and village party committee) of Xiaogang village, leaders of the all-round responsibility system and villager representatives. After listening to others' speeches, Xi Jinping delivered an important speech pointing out that Xiaogang village was the main point of origin of China's rural reform and that it was of special significance to hold the workshop in Xiaogang village. The picture above shows General Secretary Xi Jinping in a high-standard model farmland area in Xiaogang village during his investigation in Anhui

The household contract responsibility system was kept by Chen Tingyuan who went to Xiaogang many times afterwards to help them solve problems. Throughout 1979, Fengyang county implemented the all-round responsibility system while Xiaogang village fixed farm output quotas for each household.

Chapter 29

Province Approves Shannan Trial to Contract Output to Households

The historically significant third plenary session of the 11th central committee of the CPC was held in late 1978 which passed the *Decision on the Question of Accelerating Agricultural Development (Draft)* and *Regulations on the Work of Rural People's Communes (Trial Draft)*. The rural policies determined at the session tallied with the requirements of most areas nationwide, namely, to contract work quotas to groups and to link payment with production; however, under the prevailing circumstances, two 'forbids' were still defined: it was forbidden to divide up fields and go it alone, and it was forbidden to fix farm output quotas for each household. The opposition against Shannan fixing farm output quotas for each household constantly surged and people's letters denouncing Shannan commune for that reason were sent directly to Wan Li.

After celebrating the spring festival of 1979, Zhou Yueli, director of the Anhui province agriculture committee in charge of publicising the central committee's documents took a work team to Shannan. After reading the documents, he organised people to discuss them but received no response. The work team asked them to recall when they had experienced the best quality of life. Many people answered that their lives had never been better than when Zeng Xisheng implemented the responsibility field system because the land was contracted to households and people had freedom over production. Some farmers pleaded for implementation of the system of fixing farm output quotas for each household. One week later, Zhou Yueli submitted to the provincial party committee a report entitled *Farmers' Widespread Demand is to Contract Output to Households*.

The inscription above the door reads: the site in Xiaojing village where Comrade Wan Li held the first agricultural workshop on contracting production to each household

As early as October 1978, Wan Li had organised the report *Agricultural Remuneration Must be Linked Closely with Output* which, together with the survey reports on Weiying production team contracting production to groups and Xinjie commune contracting production to labourers, comprised a special issue inside the Xinhua News Agency. In early 1979, Wan Li sent the special issue for review, invited related experts and personages to discuss and research the findings, and sought their opinions. Wan Li invited Li Ruihuan to review it because of his good knowledge of philosophy. After reviewing it, Li Ruihuan regarded it as a vital question and indicated his agreement and support. The manuscript was published in *People's Daily* in January 1978.

Wan Li chaired the standing committee meeting of the provincial party committee in the Xiyuan meeting room of Daoxiang mansion on 6 February 1979.

During the discussion at the Anhui provincial party committee meeting, it was agreed that 'contracting production to each household is a good method'. But some attendees proposed: "The central committee's documents clearly 'prohibit contracting production to each household'. So the implementation of this method requires central committee approval."

Wan Li listens to people's views

Wang Guangyu, the provincial party committee secretary in charge of agriculture, reviewed at the meeting the case when Anhui promoted the responsibility field system in 1961. He said: "The responsibility field system did exert great influence on reviving and developing agricultural production, overcoming rural difficulties and improving farmers' livelihood. The farmers all miss the system very much and refer to it as the system of 'lifesaving fields'." Wang Guangyu advocated that the practice of contracting production to each household should be promoted step by step, and should at least be tested in places with backward production and economic difficulties.

The meeting did not reach unanimous agreement in the morning and continued in the afternoon.

Hearing others' views, Wan Li talked about his standpoint: "You comrades have given us many good suggestions concerning Shannan commune contracting production to each household. Comrade Wang Guangyu's review of the 'responsibility field system' in past years was enormously inspiring. Some comrades are still worried about contracting production to each household. It is fairly reasonable and completely understandable. Different views can help the provincial party committee to discover all the necessary information and make the right decision."

"Now I'd like to voice my opinion. The issue of contracting production to each household has been criticised in the past for dozens of years. Many cadres have been scared, have lingering fears about it and turn pale talking about 'contracting'. Nevertheless, it was probably right to criticise some of the things that were previously criticised whereas some of the things that were originally right might have been wrongly criticised. These things must be tested in practice. I advocate allowing Shannan commune to experiment with contracting production to each household. The pros outweigh the cons and merit a small-scale experiment. The experiment should not be publicised, published in newspapers or promoted for a while. We'll check the result after summarising the situation after the autumn. It will be great if the trial succeeds; it will not be a big deal if it fails; we need not fear stepping onto the capitalist road because we have the means to put it on the right track. Even if no grain is collected, the provincial party committee will be responsible for allocating grain for people to eat."

Province Approves Shannan Trial to Contract Output to Households

Worn-out furniture attests to the poor lives of Shannan farmers

In 1978, Wan Li labours together with farmers on an inspection tour of the countryside in Changfeng county, Anhui province

Xiaojing village in Anhui, the cradle of contracting production to each household in rural China

Wan Li's suggestion was unanimously agreed by the participants. The meeting finally decided to have a trial in Shannan commune in Feixi county. Supported by Wan Li and the provincial party committee, Shannan commune in Feixi county contracted all the cultivated land to the households.

During 14-20 February 1979, the CPC Fengyang county committee held a work meeting to profoundly discuss the practice of 'rewards linked to production' and other forms of the production responsibility system in Mahu commune.

After a heated debate, the attendees both affirmed that 'rewards linked to production' were better than 'headlong mass action' and pointed out that the specific methods were too complicated, onerous and difficult to manage because dozens of items had to be taken into consideration to fix the work and many accounts had to be calculated for distribution. They believed a production team should be divided up into several groups for separate operations and accounting. What should be turned over to the state and the collective should be done as it was due and the rest should be distributed by the groups. Such a method was considered to be easier and more feasible than 'rewards linked to production'. This was the all-round responsibility system summarised by Chen Yingyuan.

Xiaojing village as it looks today

The new spacious, bright, tidy and practical houses of Xiaojing villagers

After listening to the report of Wang Yuzhao and Chen Tingyuan one week later, Wan Li said: "Let's give it a chance", "My only fear is that production may not be increased. It will be OK as long as the production is increased."

Contracting all-round responsibility to the teams won the ardent support of farmers throughout the county. They competed to sign agreements with the production teams on contracting all-round responsibility. Raising the money for weddings, building houses, food, clothing and loans, they rushed to buy fertilisers, farm implements and seeds, and threw themselves into spring ploughing and production in 1979.

Chapter 30

Enormous Pressure from Beijing

On 15 March 1979, the *People's Daily* published 'a letter from Zhang Hao' and a related editor's note in a front-page headline saying that "we cannot retreat from the system based on the team and the places contracting production to the group and dividing up fields among groups must be firmly rectified". The author of the letter was named Zhang Hao. Later, the matter was called 'the Zhang Hao incident'.

Zhang Hao did not write the letter himself and the letter was sent to the newspaper office with the approval of a central committee leader in charge of agriculture. 'Firm rectification' was chiefly targeted at Anhui. Anhui stood at the forefront of the acute struggle and Wan Li also faced enormous pressure.

On 15 March 1979, the *People's Daily* published 'a letter from Zhang Hao' with a front-page headline

Not only was the group-based production (contract) system being implemented across a large expanse of Anhui but also the household-based production system was being developed in some areas. If contracting output to the group was not allowed, it would be impossible to contract to each household. Tension prevailed throughout the province, people sensed that the letter 'came right from the top' and cadres were worried they would be punished; people felt the policies would change and did not want to put in more effort; some communes slowed down to gauge the 'tendency'; large scale 'rectification' occurred in some individual places.

CPC Anhui provincial committee secretary Wan Li was in Hefei when he heard the news from the morning broadcast. The first thing that came to his mind was that: "It's too bad! It is contrary to the 'six articles'. The news criticised Anhui." Wan Li immediately called up CPC Chuxian county prefectural committee secretary Wang Yuzhao and said: "We should do what we need to do. We can't change a policy we have already implemented."

The next day, Wan Li set out and successively came to Lai'an, Quanjiao and Dingyuan, stablising the mood of cadres and people there as he went. Wherever he went, he repeatedly stressed: "The responsibility system was approved by the provincial party committee which will be responsible for any problem." "We should finish what we started, we should not waver."

A county leader said: "It seems that the central committee does not approve of our practice here." Wan Li responded: "Ideas geared to people's fundamental and long-term interests should be tested through practice. We should not back down just because of a reader's letter and an editor's note. If the people's enthusiasm is frustrated, production declines and farmers starve, who will take responsibility? Your county party committee or the newspaper office? The newspaper office will not feed you."

Wang Guangyu, deputy secretary of the CPC Anhui provincial party committee in charge of agriculture, rushed to Feixi to calm the situation. He said: "You can continue with what you are doing. I can tell you that Secretary Wan Li supports you and that the 20 standing committee members of the provincial party committee will also back you up. You can implement the household-based contract system without fear as long as the farmers can have enough good food to eat."

In mid-March, the CPC Anhui provincial committee issued eight emergency 'telegrams' requiring all the local governments to be unswervingly stable and to focus their energy on spring ploughing and production, regardless of what sort of responsibility system they were adopting.

On 16 March, provincial party committee secretary Wang Guangyu came to Fengyang. Chen Tingyuan promptly reported his own viewpoint and won Wang Guangyu's approval. He said: "Chen, keep doing what you're doing and let things proceed!" Wan Li called him up that very night: "Don't make any changes and let's test it in practice. We will continue with it next year if production increases this year." The CPC Chuxian county prefectural committee also phoned to show their support.

Chen Tingyuan told his superiors of his determination: "The spring ploughing and production has begun and the all-round responsibility system cannot be changed. Now I'm like Wang Xiao'er building a pigsty - firmly insisting on my faith."

Wan Li reaffirmed the daring measures of the CPC Anhui provincial committee

With the support of Wan Li, Lu Jiafeng, a cadre of the Anhui province agriculture committee, wrote an article in the *People's Daily* to counterattack Zhang Hao's letter

On 30 March 1979, the *People's Daily* published *Correctly Treating the Responsibility System Linked to Output* prominently on the front page to criticise the views in the letter *'The Team-Based Three-level Ownership' Should be Stablised* carried in the *People's Daily* on 15 March.

The article was written, arranged and organised personally by CPC Anhui provincial party committee secretary Wan Li. Wan Li told the prefectural and county leaders steadfastly: "The newspapers do not till the land nor thresh grain. If the farmers do not have food to eat after the autumn harvest, they will turn to us for help! Let's leave things alone and carry on with what we are doing!"

Different from the daring measures of the CPC Anhui provincial committee, the leaders of the CPC Feixi county committee were very prudent. To prevent the expansion of production contracted to each household, they made a decision not to allow that system. To avoid conflict with the decision of the provincial party committee, they decided that Shannan commune would not be restricted by that decision.

A storm was brewing. The county party committee repeatedly suggested rectifying the practice of contracting production to each household. Some local governments adopted tough measures to 'rectify' the practice and commune members rose up to oppose them by means of boycotting ploughing and planting. Because the standing committee of the provincial party committee "had decided not to use force to stop the production contracted to households that had already been implemented", the county party committee hurriedly put a stop to its 'rectification'.

The Feixi county magistrate said: "More than 20 central committee leaders in charge of the party and political institutions and the people in charge of 23 provinces and cities nationwide came to investigate production contracted to each household in Feixi in 1979. Some approved but others shook their heads. As a consequence, I was puzzled what to do next."

As to that disturbance, Wan Li once said: "I even wanted to hang myself in the severest difficulties." In the tensest situation, Wan Li dialled the number of the house of an old comrade in Beijing. The phone rang for quite a while but nobody answered it. It was a meaningful political signal.

Wan Li was mentally prepared. One evening, he was walking with his wife Bian Tao and told her: "Our production contracted to each household has progressed rapidly. The situation is tense in Beijing. If something disastrous happens to me, please take good care of our children."

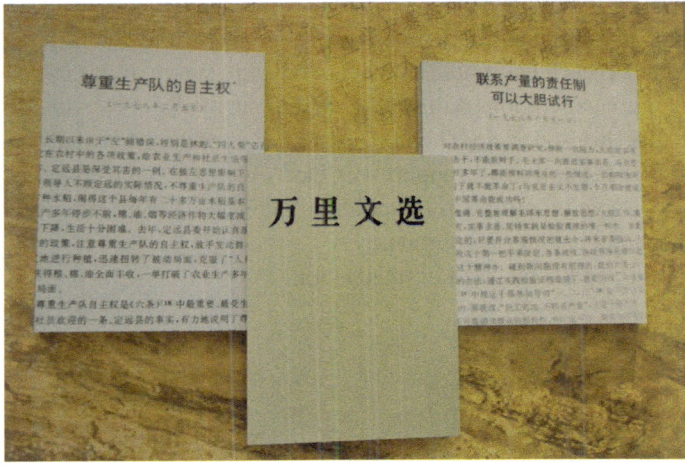

Some articles discussing the autonomous rights and the responsibility system for rural production in the *Selected Works of Wan Li*

Wan Li and his wife Bian Tao on the Great Wall at Badaling in the winter of 1972

Bian Tao replied: "That's scary, isn't it?"

Wan Li said: "Political struggles have always been cruel and ruthless. You didn't expect that I would be toppled twice before."

Bian Tao murmured: "Yes, I know."

When his children went to visit him in Anhui, Wan Li told them: "I won't consider my personal gains or losses in a bid to implement production contracted to each household so that nobody will starve. It doesn't matter if I die. Future generations will surely rehabilitate me."

At this, his son Wan Zhongxiang felt excited and hurriedly told his father: "Your family will support you. Don't worry about us. We've grown up and we live on our own. It wouldn't matter if we were taken as family members of a counter-revolutionary."

Wan Li nodded his head in satisfaction.

Chapter 31

Lao Chen, You Have My Approval To Do This for Three To Five Years

At 9 o'clock on the morning of 21 May 1979, Wan Li went to Shannan commune to inspect its work in person. He did not listen to the report but asked the commune leaders some questions.

Wan: Do you have fears about what you are doing?
Wang: No.
Wan: Really?
Wang: It's hard not to be a little afraid.
Wan: Afraid of what?

Wan Li (left) listens to farmers' views on contracting production to each household (part of a bronze sculpture)

Wang: Afraid that someone might say we're divorced from three-level ownership based on teams.

Wan: What else?

Wang: I fear that unified accounting and distribution would not be feasible.

Wan: You can rest assured about it. I'm here now. The provincial party committee knows you are conducting experiments here with my approval. We can summarise our experience in the autumn.

Wan Li asked in detail about the harvest, requisitioning by purchase, collective accumulation, animal breeding, water conservancy construction, the five guarantees and welfare. Only a dozen people were originally invited to attend the workshop in the afternoon. But people rushed to attend it after they heard that Secretary Wan was presiding over the workshop.

In the face of people's surprise and joy, Wan Li frankly asked: "What's your view on what you are doing now? I'm here ready to listen to your views. So please don't hesitate to air your views and questions."

Li Zuzhong, an accountant with the Xiaojing production team,

The site of the workshop on contracting production to each household held in Xiaojing village

asked: "Secretary Wan, do the higher authorities (referring to the central committee) approve of contracting production to each household?"

Wan Li dodged the question about the central committee document 'not permitting production to be contracted to each household' and conveyed his firm support: "Go ahead, the provincial party committee is always behind you."

"We are a little afraid," said some people.

"Afraid of what?" Wan Li asked.

"Afraid of change," answered several people simultaneously.

"Is contracting production to each household good or not?" Wan Li asked, changing the subject.

"It's good. In the 60 years I've lived, I've never seen wheat grow so well," answered an old man in his sixties.

"Contracting production to each household is far better than 'headlong mass action' and if we carry on doing it for several years we'll have plenty of food to eat," continued someone else.

"Nothing is going to change. You can continue doing it for years," Wan Li promised resolutely and decisively.

"Secretary Wan, could you please give us a definite answer as to how many years?" a canny middle-aged man asked.

"Still not convinced?" Wan Li asked smilingly. "You can continue doing it as long as you like." He paused for a moment and said solemnly: "But you should protect communal facilities and public property such as warehouses and cowsheds and should not harm the collective economy. Contracting production to each household is aimed at increasing production and making enough good food for people!"

Before his departure, Wan Li said with emotion: "I'll come back to see you after the autumn harvest."

In the summer of 1979, Shannan was blessed with a bumper harvest. The people of Shannan commune planted a total of more than 1,300 hectares of collective and private wheat with a gross output of some 2,500 tonnes, an increase of more than 1,500 tonnes compared with previous years. Consequently the superiority of production contracted to each household was shown. "Nobody can stop the tendency of contracting production to each household in Shannan." By the summer of 1979, more than 2,600

In December 1978, the people of Tianchang county, Anhui province overcame the most severe drought in a century to achieve a bumper grain harvest

production teams throughout Feixi county had implemented the system of contracting production to each household, accounting for over one third (37.1%) of the total.

On 5 June 1979, Wan Li came to Fengyang and Chen Tingyuan gave him a report on contracting production to each household: The all-round responsibility system was simple, guaranteeing what is turned over to the state and the collective and leaving the rest to ourselves. Now more than 80% of farmers' households in Fengyang county have implemented production contracted to each household.

Wan Li asked: "What is the effect of contracting production to each household?"

Chen Tingyuan quoted what the farmers of Fengyang said: "The all-round responsibility system is so good that both the cadres and the people want to implement it. As long as we work hard for three to five years, we will store grain to eat and grass to burn. The individuals and the collective will become rich and the state will build more granaries."

On hearing the report delivered in such vivid and entertaining rhyming couplets, Wan Li smiled happily and declared on the spot: "Lao Chen, you have my approval to continue for three to five more years."

Chen Tingyuan said: "Now the people are really afraid of making mistakes and of possible changes."

Wan Li answered: "They won't make mistakes and I'll be responsible for them if any. The problem is whether you can improve production and whether the commune members can get rich."

"Now some people criticise us for our 'three-and-half-level accounting."

Wan Li replied: "As long as production is improved, there is nothing to be afraid of. Whether accounting is done on three-and-a-half or four levels, it's all socialist in nature. If households also implement economic accounting, isn't it five-level accounting? Production, operations and management all need to be accounted for economically. No matter what form of responsibility system is adopted, as long as it helps to improve production and increase the incomes of farmers, the collectives and the state, then it's a good method. That is what's important."

Chapter 32

Registering for Production Contracted to Each Household

Wan Li faced the greatest pressure in 1979. Wan Li recalled the tough thought processes when he met a scholar on the party's history in 1997.

Wan Li had a difference of opinion in discussing the *Decision of the CPC Central Committee on the Question of Accelerating Agricultural Development (Draft)* in November 1978. The draft mentioned 'three cans' and 'two forbids' (the 'three cans' are: can calculate work points according to quotas, can calculate work points according to a review of hours worked and can contract work to work groups, link payment for work with production, and reward overproduction under the premise of unified accounting and distribution of the production team; the 'two forbids' are: forbid dividing up fields and going it alone, and forbid contracting production to each household). Wan Li said: "I agree to continue to have the three 'cans' that can emancipate people's minds and give farmers a free hand; the two 'forbids' are not aligned with that spirit and should be eliminated. But the leaders in charge of formulating the draft did not accept my viewpoint."

Wan Li proposed again to cancel the two 'forbids' before the document was passed at the fourth plenary session of the 11th central committee of the CPC in September 1979 but his proposal was rejected. Wan Li specially went to talk about it with Comrade Yaobang (Hu Yaobang) and seriously proposed: "Let's delete 'forbiding the contracting of production to each household' in the document!" Yaobang replied: "The drafters do not agree. I need to work more on that."

Wan Li said: "Later I knew that before the official publication of the document, the central committee changed the two 'forbids' into one 'forbid' and one 'don't', namely: prohibit dividing up fields and going it alone, and don't implement production contracted to each household apart from cases of special needs for sideline production and some single families suffering from inconvenient transportation in remote mountainous areas. The modification distinguished between the two and made an exception for production contracted to each household. It was definitely progressive compared with the originally published *Draft* but the conflicts were not completely worked out."

"Neither 'forbid' nor 'don't' allowed production to be contracted to each household. However, it had been implemented in Anhui. When Fengyang generally contracted all-round responsibility to the teams, some villages also contracted production to households. The production contracted to each household was applied secretly at the very beginning in Xiaogang in Fengyang. The county party committee secretary Chen Tingyuan discovered it first. But he helped them hide it from the higher authorities rather than the lower authorities, and even the prefectural party committee did not know about it. I knew about it later, turned a blind eye to it and encouraged it during my inspection. Some kind-hearted comrades reflected to me that someone criticised that our action went against the constitution and the party's decision."

Deng Xiaoping met leaders in charge of the CPC Anhui provincial committee and the CPC Huizhou prefectural committee in Huangshan in July 1979; the fourth from left in the front row is Wan Li

The third plenary session of the 11th central committee of the CPC held in December 1978 was the greatest and most significant turning in the party's history since the founding of the PRC. The picture shows Deng Xiaoping and Chen Yun in the meeting

"How to deal with it? I said the farmers were for it and determined to apply it. They can summon up courage and stick it out since they've started. I cannot publicly oppose the party's decision not to allow production to be contracted to each household. But I said to them: 'You did it with my approval. You can continue doing it and I'll be responsible for any possible problem.' Anhui's 'violation of the law and discipline' in essence reflected the conflicts between the farmers' need to develop productivity and the inflexible superstructure and old regulations."

That year it was Deng Xiaoping's and Chen Yun's words that really bolstered Wan Li's confidence. When he attended the second session of the fifth National People's Congress in June 1979, Wan Li reported to Deng Xiaoping the promotion of the responsibility system in Anhui and the pressure from all aspects. Hearing Wan Li's report, Deng Xiaoping pointed out: "There's no question about it. You should carry on doing it."

Registering for Production Contracted to Each Household

Also during that session, Wan Li talked about Anhui's agriculture with Comrade Chen Yun. Chen Yun said: "I totally agree with Anhui's reform."

Wan Li felt happiest in 1979 because he repeatedly asked Fengyang party committee and Shannan party committee to deliver some achievements. By the end of the year, 8,189 production teams throughout Feixi county had contracted production to each household, accounting for 97% of the total. The system also brought a bumper harvest of agricultural production. The output of grain for the whole year totalled 377,000 tonnes, 127,000 tonnes of which were turned over to the state, more than three times the amount in 1978 and putting an end to the long history of being fed on resold grain by the state.

The year 1979 witnessed an unprecedented bumper harvest in Xiaogang village as a result of contracting production to each household. The gross output of food grain that year was equivalent to the total output during the five years from 1966 to 1970. The total output of oil and grain was equivalent to the total amount produced over the past 20 years. The grain turned over to the state was 10 times the target while the sale of oil-bearing plants exceeded the target by 80 times. Xiaogang village changed from a 'village of beggars' to an 'outstanding village'.

On 7 October 2008, Shen Hao (second from right), secretary of the CPC Xiaogang village party branch and the leaders of the all-round responsibility system including Guan Youjiang, Yan Junchang, Yan Jinchang and Yan Xuechang exchange information about reform in Xiaogang village

On 1 January 1980, the CPC Anhui provincial committee held a provincial agricultural conference at which Chen Tingyuan delivered a field survey report on Xiaogang entitled *An Indispensable Tonic - Survey on the Production Contracted to Xiaogang Production Team of Liyuan Commune in Fengyang County* which deeply moved Wan Li.

On 3 January 1980, the Anhui rural work conference was officially held. At the very beginning, Wan Li did not give a long speech but only said: "We are hold this meeting on the third day of the year (1980) simply to ask you to draw on the practice of the last two years, jointly discuss the problems and find a route and a policy to develop agriculture correctly."

Hardly had his voice faded away when a debate occurred on the all-round responsibility system and on contracting production to each household. Those who approved of the practice said: "The practice of more than one year proves that the production team is inferior to the group which in turn is inferior to the household. All the production contracted to households increased in terms of output and income. Some described it as going it alone. What if it is going it alone? It is only working alone and doesn't change its socialist nature at all." Those who objected to the practice held the view that: "It's not conceivable that the all-round responsibility system and contracting production to each household are always good without exception. Surely there must be a few problems in Chuxian county?"

The CPC Anhui provincial committee prepared a draft summary for the meeting and submitted it for discussion and modification. The attendees either agreed to or opposed the draft summary. Those against it thought that "the draft summary was a retrogressive declaration and that those drafting it should be unmasked" and even proposed to "reorganise the secretariat of the meeting".

The opponents also said: "Lower-level cadres believed that the 'two cans' advocated by Comrade Wan Li were just the 'two forbids' in the central committee's document and that because his advocacy was oral rather than written, it shows that he acted in a slippery way and that he himself is also afraid." The proponents of the practice took the view that: "Production contracted to each household can be implemented in not merely two or three years and the fact that it is contracted to individuals need not be a secret. Our minds should be emancipated." Wang Yuzhao suggested: "Let's give a legal identity to the all-round responsibility system and acknowledge that it is a form of socialist production responsibility system."

On 11 January, Wan Li made vigorous efforts to turn the tide and his resonant voice reverberated around the meeting room: "Why has contracting production to each household aroused such a heated debate? We have undertaken it for years from the very beginning and reports about it flooded in when we began to formulate the 'six articles'. Some kind-hearted people have called on me not to make mistakes which has been a lingering fear."

"The word 'contract' is a good thing so don't be afraid of it. In circumstances whereby the economy has long been backward, the collective economy has been mismanaged, and ultra-leftist thinking has caused severe disruption and punishment, and made people's lives destitute, people have become accustomed to a small-peasant economy for historical and class reasons. Contracting production to each household is not something advocated by us. It is like a baby whose mother is happy about its birth. Thank goodness! It solves the problem. Let's give it a legal identity. The baby is good. Many people go to see it with utmost enthusiasm but feel terribly disheartened. Why? Because it is illegal and open to criticism. But I don't agree with that idea."

Anhui provincial leaders attend the inauguration ceremony for the 'All-round responsibility system memorial' of Xiaogang village inscribed by Wan Li

An old thatched cottage in Xiaogang village kept for the enlightenment and education of future generations

A view of Xiaogang village as it looks today

Wan Li clearly affirmed in his speech that 'contracting production to each household' was a socialist production responsibility system. He said: "Contracting production to each household is different from dividing up fields and going it alone. If the latter means the collapse of the collective economy and a return to individual ownership and individual management by farmers, contracting production to each household does not have that problem. It is still a production system that contracts responsibility to the household. It is socialist rather than capitalist in nature."

Wan Li added: "There are many diverse types of responsibility system. Contracting production to each household is also a responsibility system linking payment with production, which should be allowed to coexist rather than be removed in a sweeping approach."

Xiaogang village cadres on a study tour of Xigou village, Pingshun county, Shanxi province in 2008 accompanied by national model worker Shen Jilan (first from right)

In the company of Chen Tingyuan on 24 January, Wan Li visited a series of households in Xiaogang and saw that all their grain containers were full of grain. Some of the grain was piled up in the courtyard if there was not enough space in the storage rooms.

Wan Li was very happy about this and said to Xiaogang production team leader Yan Junchang: "The situation will surely take a turn for the better if you continue with it. I plan to implement the system but only fear that nobody will dare to do it. I will give you my support for doing it." When Wan Li was about to leave, the people wanted to give him some peanuts as gifts. They said there had been no peanuts to give him in the past although they had wanted to but that he should take some now since they had plenty. Wan Li wore military clothes that day with the pockets full of peanuts. When he returned and held a standing committee meeting, he put the peanuts on the table and said they were the fruits of production contracted to each household.

Chapter 33

Central Committee Issues Document No. 75 in 1980

In the spring of 1980, Wan Li was transferred to work in the central committee and acted as secretary of the central committee secretariat and vice premier of the state council in charge of agriculture. Wan Li said: "Although I'm not living in Zhongnanhai, I will not sleep well until the people shake off poverty." At that time, there prevailed a rhyming couplet 'if you want to eat rice, look for Wan Li' (this rhymes in Chinese: *yao chi mi, zhao wan li*).Once Wan Li started working in the central committee in charge of agriculture, agricultural reform should have been accelerated. However, that was not the case.

Group photo of CPC central committee secretariat members in 1981. From left: Xi Zhongxun, Fang Yi, Gu Mu, Yang Dezhi, Hu Yaobang, Wan Li, Yao Yilin, Yu Qiuli and Wang Renzhong

A ballad praising Wan Li voicing the aspirations of the people of Xiaogang - the rhyming couplet reads: 'if you want to eat rice, look for Wan Li'

The agricultural committee at that time was still shackled by 'learning from Dazhai for agricultural growth' and unscrupulously blamed the all-round responsibility system and contracting production to each household in Anhui. Wan Li said: "In those years, some agricultural department leaders believed that contracting production to each household was destroying the collective economy, hindered mechanisation and led to inadequate irrigation. I worked as the concurrent agricultural committee director and not many agricultural committee leaders really understood what was going on." Additionally, few provincial and municipal leaders supported contracting production to each household for the simple reason that the central committee's document expressly stipulated 'not to implement it'.

Comrade Chen Yun supported Wan Li. After Wan Li returned to Beijing, Chen Yun met him and said happily, taking him by the hand: "Comrade Wan Li, I totally agree with the methods you are using (referring to contracting production to each household) in Anhui's rural areas."

In April 1980, the CPC central committee held a meeting on the long-term economic development plan. Deng Xiaoping pointed out at the meeting that some rural areas with backward production and difficult economies in Gansu, Inner Mongolia, Yunnan and Guizhou should implement 'contracting production to each household'. In May, Deng Xiaoping clearly pointed out in the discussion of *Questions Concerning Rural Policy* that: "After rural policy was relaxed, some places suitable for production contracted to each household implemented the system which brought about good results and rapid changes. An absolute majority of the production teams in Feixi county, Anhui province implemented contracting production to each household which drastically increased production. Most production teams in Fengyang county, accustomed to singing the 'Fengyang flower drum' song (performed by beggars in this traditionially impoverished rural area of Anhui), implemented contracting production to each household and took on a new look in just one year. Some comrades are worried that the system might affect the collective economy. But I don't think of it as a problem." "Generally speaking, the main problem impeding rural work is that people's minds are not adequately emancipated." "It is very important to start from the specific local conditions and the people's wishes." (*Selected Works of Deng Xiaoping*, vol. 2, pp315, 316). His affirmation for contracting production to each household and the all-round responsibility system tremendously advanced the contract responsibility system for agricultural production.

Wan Li and Deng Xiaoping chat informally

Comrade Chen Yun supported Wan Li

Wan Li said: "Comrade Xiaoping made an important speech and highly praised the contracting of production to each household in Feixi and Fengyang. Afterwards, the situation turned for the better but the argument nationwide did not stop. Some opponents are in positions of power and you cannot do it without their approval."

Central Committee Issues Document No. 75 in 1980

The central committee decided on 31 May 1980 to hold a workshop for first provincial committee secretaries in September. Wan Li invited Du Runsheng, secretary general of the rural work department during the time of Deng Zihui (a strong proponent of agricultural reform in the early 1960s), who had much practical experience, a high theoretical level and was good at handling all aspects of relationships.

Wan Li said: "I invited him to take charge of drafting and interpreting the meeting documents. I originally meant to change 'don't contract production to each household' to 'can contract production to each household' or 'support contracting production to each household'. But amid heated debate at the meeting, it seemed the motions would not be carried. A minority of the attendees stood up and publicly agreed, including Chi Biqing from Guizhou, Zhou Hui from Inner Mongolia and Ren Zhongyi from Liaoning; but most of them kept silent and the rest were firmly opposed to it."

On 3 October 1995, Wan Li revisited Fengyang, one of the points of origin of China's rural reform. This group photo shows Wan Li, Hui Liangyu who was then the CPC Anhui provincial committee secretary (first row, seventh from left) and other leaders of Fengyang county

The provincial party committee secretaries speaking out against the contracting of production to each household came from Fujian, Jiangsu and Heilongjiang while supporters of the motion came from Guizhou, Inner Mongolia and Liaoning.

Yang Yichen, first CPC Heilongjiang provincial committee secretary, and Chi Biqing, his counterpart from Guizhou, articulated the arguments for and against contracting production to each household likening them to taking a 'perfectly normal road' or a 'single-plank wooden bridge'.

Chi Biqing said that in his locality "there are not three feet of flat land and a family does not have three grams of silver" and that if they were forced to abandon contracting production to each household, it would cut off their escape route (access to their 'Huarong pass'). Yang Yichen countered: "Heilongjiang is an area with the highest level of mechanisation nationwide. Contracting production to each household will affect the development of mechanisation. Production will be seriously hindered and set back; the collective economy is the surest path and should not be aborted." Chi Biqing responded: "You can go your way and I'll go mine. Our impoverished area should go its own way!"

Wan Li said: "After repeated discussion, we finally approved a compromise document, namely, the central committee's (1980) document no. 75 entitled: *On Further Strengthening and Improving Several Issues Concerning the Agricultural Production Responsibility System*. Casting a veil over the question of whether contracting production to each household was socialist or capitalist, the document related many advantages of the practice, concurrently pointed out possible problems arising from contracting production to each household and stressed the importance of carefully preventing and promptly resolving such problems. The document greatly supported and encouraged farmers. For the communist party leadership not to have had a mass viewpoint, not to have understood the real will of the masses and not to have respected the needs of the masses would not have been the right course of action. For these reasons, contracting production to each household gradually became a wave of nationwide reform."

The minutes of the meeting pointed out: due to the characteristics of agricultural development and imbalances in regional economic development, the management of agricultural production needs to be more adaptable and flexible, and the production responsibility system ought not to adopt only one method or to adopt a sweeping approach. Specific policies and regulations concerning the scope of contracting production to each household were made: "Some production teams in remote mountainous regions and poor or backward areas are fed on resold grain, depending on loans for production and living on relief. So people have lost confidence in the collective economy and therefore require the stability of contracting production to each household for quite a long time." The regulations allowed the scope of contracting production to each household to be extended based on those of 1979. In addition, the policies were more flexible. As a consequence, production contracted to each household gradually expanded and rapidly developed.

Since the rapid development of contracting production to each household was still under suspicion and censure, it was also a topic of heated debate in theoretical circles. The central committee took a prudent attitude, on the one hand, sending investigation teams to conduct in-depth investigations in rural areas and discussing the theoretical arguments; on the other hand, carefully observing the development of the situation and finally determining right and wrong according to the development of the productive forces.

The central committee's policy at that time stipulated that: "Since the masses have contracted production to each household, there is no need to directly overturn or to antagonise the masses. To act in such a way would not promote socialist or individual enthusiasm and would negatively impact production." The starting point of the central committee was to protect the farmers' interests and enthusiasm, and the development of the productive forces. It was quite correct and objectively supported the development of contracting production to each household. By early November 1980, 15% of production teams nationwide had implemented contracting production

Chapter 34

100 Leaders in Charge of Agriculture Investigate the Rural Areas

When rural reform was flourishing comprehensively, Wan Li set out to solve the problem whereby the central committee leaders in charge of agriculture disapproved of the contract responsibility system. On 11 March 1983, Wan Li came to the Ministry of Agriculture and severely criticised the work at the previous stage and some leaders by name at the party group meeting.

In September 1981, Wan Li inspects the Sanjiang plain in Heilongjiang province seriously afflicted by flooding, familiarises himself with the disaster circumstances and shows his support for workers and staff of the 5910 farm fourth branch and officers and men of the PLA providing disaster relief

Wan Li continued: "Some comrades did not consider the fundamental interests of the farmers and the relationship between the party and the farmers nor the reasons why the farmers have not had enough food to eat for 30 years. Now we have hope for change. But they cannot accept it and feel worried instead. I'm afraid these comrades only have an abstract image of farmers and ignore the farmers on the edge of starvation."

"The principles of one responsibility system, one autonomous right and one material interest – these three issues – refer to the responsibility, right and interest that we so often talk about. However loudly the slogan of socialism is shouted, it becomes an empty word if these three issues are not properly resolved or are not linked with people's interests. In the final analysis, it is 'leftist' talk intent on making mischief. It is not the existence but the degree of 'leftist' thinking that distinguishes our comrades. It is permissible to have divergent views but not for people to arbitrarily go their own way. The Ministry of Agriculture is a department of the state council. In the past the whole nation learnt from Dazhai, but now even Dazhai is changing. How can the department leading the campaign to learn from Dazhai not adapt better to the changed situation?"

"Now that farmers have been given a free hand, many new problems are waiting to be resolved and urgently need improved leadership. It is quite different from the past practice of encouraging grain planting. How can you lead farmers when you give arbitrary orders?"

In November 1985, Wan Li investigates the old Yimengshan revolutionary base area in Shandong while the masses gather round to offer him peanuts they have produced on their own plots

Wan Li (second from right) and Hu Qili (first from right) investigating Xiguan brigade, Chengguan commune, Muping county, Shandong province in February 1984, happy to see a telephone installed in a commune member's house

Wan Li talking about domestic affairs and becoming rich with the family of Liu Cunde (second from right), a key cattle raiser of the Hui nationality during an inspection tour in the eastern part of Ping'an county, Qinghai province in July 1984

100 Leaders in Charge of Agriculture Investigate the Rural Areas

In August 1983, Wan Li and Li Peng visit Ankang district in Shaanxi province which was severely afflicted by flooding to offer the masses their condolences on behalf of the CPC central committee and the state council

In September 1995, Wan Li inspects what was known during the revolutionary war years as the Hebei-Shandong-Henan border area and southwest Shandong (now Heze city, Shandong province). The photo shows Wan Li learning about the production situation of papayas, a special local product of Heze

In 1982, Wan Li chats with a Mongolian herdsman

"Our immediate concerns are, first, to improve farmers' livelihoods and, second, to increase the agricultural commodity rate. With regard to farmers only being able to practice commodity exchange - a fundamental problem is how to help farmers get rich as soon as possible and how to provide more commodities. This is not just an agricultural issue. There is no way out for our country unless we develop a commodity economy."

Finally, Wan Li suggested that leaders in charge of agricultural departments go to look at villages in person. He said: 'Some people draw their salaries, eat their fill, rely on old experiences and subjective impressions, and stay in Beijing while pontificating on issues – that's not the right way to proceed. They should all go and investigate in person, go and take a look for themselves, otherwise it's very difficult for them to unify their ideological understanding."

In accordance with Wan Li's instructions, in early April, the state agriculture commission organised more than 100 leaders in charge of agricultural departments into 17 separate investigation teams to investigate the contract responsibility systems in 15 priority provinces and regions. Wan Li's speech made a great impact on them. Although most of the comrades participating in the investigation were more than 50 years old and some even 70 years old, they spared no pains to hold a workshop at the frontline of agriculture, talked sincerely with farmers household by household and obtained an enormous amount of first-hand information.

In late June, the state agriculture commission held a series of three workshops to listen to their reports. Going to the rural areas for investigation broadened their horizons and had a leapfrog-effect on their views about Chinese villages and farmers. Their reports were vivid and they generally reflected that they had enhanced their awareness, unified their thinking, found out about some problems and obtained a lot of first-hand information.

After he learnt about this, Wan Li said: "After criticising them last time, I've been paying a lot of attention to them. Despite their advanced age, I sent them to experience the tough environment on the front line of agriculture which proved to be the best and most effective method. They are all central committee leaders in charge of agricultural departments and their mentality will exert an important influence on the overall rural reform process."

Chapter 35

Five Central Committee No. 1 Documents Issued in Succession

When he was in charge of agriculture, Wan Li held a rural work conference at the end of every year and issued a central committee no. 1 document at the beginning of each year from 1981 to 1986. For five years in succession, the central committee issued policies and measures concerning rural reform in the form of 'no. 1 documents', which was rare in the CPC's history and reflected the serious attention paid by the CPC central committee to rural reform under Wan Li's direction. It was precisely the five 'no. 1 documents' that continuously deepened rural reform and facilitated the earthshaking changes in China's countryside.

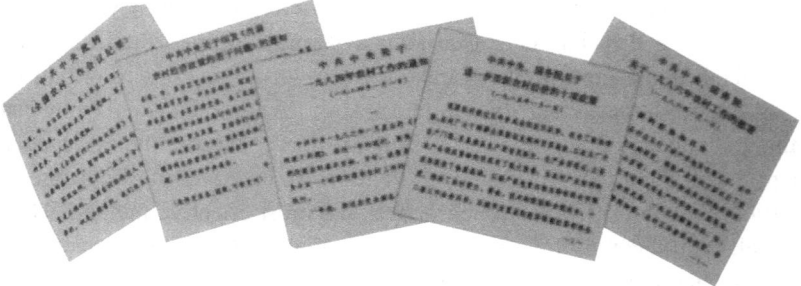

The central committee's five 'no. 1 documents'

Under the historic conditions prevailing in late 1981, there were still some people within the party and within the country that could not completely accept the innovations arising out of the reforms and regarded 'contracting production to each household' as a capitalist practice of dividing up fields and going it alone. For this reason, it was of critical importance to determine whether contracting production to each household was capitalist or socialist. The CPC central committee issued the first 'no. 1 document' entitled *Nationwide Rural Work Conference Minutes* on agricultural issues on 1 January 1982.

The document clearly pointed out that contracting responsibility to each household and the all-round responsibility system were 'all socialist production responsibility systems'. Concurrently the document clarified that it was 'not to be confused with the previous individual economy of petty private ownership but that it was an integral component of the socialist agricultural economy'.

Wan Li at a meeting talking about farmers and rural reform

That conclusion was of critical importance. Incorporating the contracting of production to each household within the scope of the socialist economy was a big deal in terms of settling the argument on the nature of the system, and changing the previous 'temporary permission' into an 'official permit' of its socialist nature, thereby putting farmers' minds at ease and legalising its promotion.

The document was submitted to the central committee before being issued and won Deng Xiaoping's 'total approval'. Chen Yun specially asked his secretary to call up and said: "It is a good document that can win the support of the cadres and the people."

The document dispelled any lingering doubts in people's minds so that there was a flurry of activity. By late 1982, 90% of teams nationwide had implemented some form of household contract responsibility system for production. Even Dazhai village, Xiyang county, Shanxi province which had persistently criticised 'contracting production to each household' as capitalism became restless.

In 1983 the central committee's second 'no. 1 document' entitled *Questions About Current Rural Economic Policy* was issued and affirmed that the household contract responsibility system was a great creation of Chinese farmers under the CPC's leadership. It put forward 'two transformations', namely, to encourage transformation from a self-sufficient or semi-self-sufficient agricultural economy to large-scale commercial production and to transform from traditional agriculture to modern agriculture. Moreover, the document pointed out that theoretically the household contract responsibility system was 'a great creation of Chinese farmers under the CPC's leadership and a new development of Marxist theory on agricultural cooperativisation based on China's practice'.

Wan Li later recalled: "The document was smoothly approved by the central committee's secretariat. Some old comrades who had not agreed with contracting production to each household before admitted that they had felt worried because their minds had not been fully emancipated and they had not realised the huge effectiveness of the system."

The year 1983 witnessed the full implementation of the household contract responsibility system and the intensification and expansion of rural economic reform. By late 1983, the production contract responsibility systems chiefly linked to households had been implemented in more than 90% of farmers' households nationwide.

In 1979 China's total grain output was over 300 million tonnes, a new record high. The photo shows farmers in Henan getting in the summer grain harvest

In June 1987, Wan Li delivers a speech at the opening ceremony of the World Food Council's 13th Ministerial Sessions on behalf of the Chinese government

In 1984, the central committee's third 'no.1 document' entitled *Notice on Rural Work in 1984* was issued, stressing the need to further stabilise and improve the contract responsibility system and stipulating that the land contract period should generally be more than 15 years and even longer for projects with a long cycle of production or development. In the third 'no.1 document', the issue of hiring labourers did not win consensus. Deng Xiaoping said: "We should not hurry to restrict it. Let's see its achievements and talk about it in three years' time."

It was only in 1984 that China's output of grain historically broke through 400 million tonnes, up 100 million tonnes over 1978. Minister of Agriculture He Kang declared at the World Food and Agriculture Organisation Conference to the world that the Chinese government had basically solved China's subsistence problem.

In 1985, the central committee's fourth 'no.1 document' entitled *Ten Policies on Further Invigorating the Rural Economy* was issued, eliminating the system of unified purchase and purchase by state quotas of agricultural and sideline products for 30 years and stipulating the new policy of contracted and planned purchase of a minority of important products including grain and cotton by the state.

After the fourth 'no.1 document' was issued, even agricultural specialists felt worried: can the market absorb so much fruit if the state does not purchase it?"

In 1986, the central committee's fifth 'no.1 document' entitled *Deployment of Rural Work in 1986* was issued attaching priority to further enhancing the basic status of agriculture and vigorously improving conditions for agricultural production in response to such issues as rising agricultural costs and decreasing income. At that time the slogan for developing the agricultural economy was 'first, depend on policy, second, depend on science and technology'. The document added a third condition: 'third, depend on input'. The issue of agricultural input gradually came into the view of central committee decision-makers.

Experts on agriculture later evaluated: "The five 'no.1 documents' focused on: one basic plan, namely, to plan urban and rural socio-economic development; one basic guideline, namely, to have industry support agriculture, cities support villages and to implement the policy of giving more, taking less and loosening control; and one basic task, namely, to build a new socialist countryside.

Wan Li chatting informally with Peng Zhen (left) and Xi Zhongxun (right) in June 1982

The five no.1 documents introduced gradually year by year, initially: formed the new agricultural and rural policy systems to comprehensively build an affluent society for a new era; put an end to the history of more than 2,600 years whereby farmers working the land had to pay the 'imperial grain tax'; increased support and protection for agriculture, implemented a series of agricultural subsidy systems and ushered in a new era of directly subsidising farmers; explicitly shifted the focus of infrastructure construction to the villages; clearly required the newly increased general expenditure earmarked for education, health and culture to be chiefly appropriated to the rural areas; constantly protected rural migrant workers' rights and interests.

The greatest advantages of the five years lay in the continuity of policy, invigorating 'agricultural issues' and fostering the promising situation of stable agricultural development. Grain production increased for four consecutive years with total output amounting to 515 million tonnes in 2007; farmers' per capita net income exceeded Rmb4,140, an increase of more than 6% annually for four consecutive years; farmers' living standards were remarkably boosted. Rural residents' per capita net income rose from Rmb134 to Rmb4,140 in 2007, an increase of 6.3 times that in 1978, representing an annual increase of 7.1% after adjustment for price factors.

Chapter 36

Three Experiences of Rural Reform

The result of China's rural reform was decided in 1985. At the rural work conference in October that year, Wan Li summarised three experiences about rural reform. Simple and frequently discussed, these experiences were the key to successful reform and shone as a typical example of historical materialism.

The first was to adhere to the opinions of the people and respect their initiative. Wan Li said: "Why did rural reform succeed from the outset? Mainly because the central committee's policies reflected the needs of farmers, represented their interests, gave them autonomous rights and boosted their enthusiasm. Only when their enthusiasm was heightened and rural reform was invigorated could the development of the national economy be accelerated.

"Then, where did these new rural policies come from? Without doubt, they were the fruit of the collective wisdom of CPC members and the party, and administrative leaders of all levels had performed mountains of work for summarisation and enhancement. However, of greater importance were the working practices of hundreds of millions of farmers. Why did the household responsibility system break through first in poorest areas? It was primarily because farmers in poor areas suffered most from egalitarianism and arbitrary orders, and had the most to gain from reform. Both the production contracted to each household and the all-round responsibility system were adopted by the local farmers themselves. A group of rural cadres risked being punished in supporting farmers through reform, strived for the interests of farmers regardless of any personal gain and dared to break the old rules and regulations. That was the real outlook on the people and the essence to serve them wholeheartedly. Deciding how to understand and treat farmers is always a fundamental question for us in the reform."

Farmers' Daily **published a special edition entitled 'Why did China's reform break through in rural areas?'**

Wan Li laid special stress on the question of farmers. As he said, China had a population of 1bn and 800m of them were farmers. That was the fundamental reality of the country. Without keeping the farmers in mind or protecting people's political and democratic rights and economic benefits, the people would have no mass view or notion of the state and the overall situation. Additionally, claiming to serve the heart and soul of the people would be reduced to mere empty talk. China's modernisation was mostly concerned with serving the interests of farmers, who accounted for 80% of the country's population, and helping them achieve modernisation.

Wan Li working in his office

The second experience was to seek truth from facts and take practice as the sole criterion to test truth. He said it was exceedingly difficult to really seek truth from facts; the general truth and reality should be fully combined and it was crucial to know the people's wishes and requirements, evaluate the situation and forecast the trend of history based on practical work; rural reform must begin with the reality of different regions, respect the people's wishes and give a free hand to the people to choose the most suitable mode of operation in practice; the undecided mode of operation should not be simply affirmed or negated and indecisive people should not be labelled or criticised. That was the way to seek truth from facts.

If practice was not taken to be the sole criterion to test truth and only the superior authorities and theories were followed rather than the realities, production contracted to each household would not be carried out correctly. He said: "Incessant practice should answer the questions of how to build socialism and how to make policies. I firmly believe that only practice can test truth and only methods that solve practical problems are good methods."

When he reviewed the government work report with the representatives of Zhejiang province who attended the third session of the seventh NPC in March 1990, Wan Li said: 'The CPC's fundamental rural economic policy will not change and the continuity and stability of the policy will be maintained'

The third experience was to continue with reform. He pointed out the fact that farmers applied production contracted to each household despite various accusations and facing illegal pressure, which were a consequence of the fact that that the old systems and superstructure could not adapt to farmers' requirements to develop the productive forces. The most important productive forces were people. Their enthusiasm depended on whether productive relations were adapted to productive forces. The farmers' enthusiasm was driven by democratic rights and material interests, which required reforming the systems influencing their democratic rights and economic benefits.

Wan Li said that reform was aimed at opening up a road to build socialism with Chinese characteristics, accelerating the development of social productivity, gradually improving people's material and cultural lives, and achieving modernisation as soon as possible. Such reform had not been done before and it was bound to encounter difficulties, setbacks and problems. Efforts should be made to eliminate potential disturbances despite the difficulties, conduct surveys and research, depend on people's social practices to open up new ways to recognise and solve problems, boost and unify cadres' ideas in practical work and push the cause of reform ahead in a down-to-earth manner.

Chapter 37

The Important Topic of Political Restructuring

On 31 July 1986 Wan Li, who was serving as a member of the political bureau of the central committee and vice premier of the state council, made a speech at a meeting entitled 'Democratic and scientific decision-making is an important topic of political restructuring'. Later, Wan Li sent the speech to Deng Xiaoping and Chen Yun for review. After reviewing it, Deng Xiaoping did not change a single word and wrote the following instruction: "Good, publish it in full." Chen Yun also wrote an instruction: "The speech solved a vital problem that has not been settled by our party for so many years."

In March 1986, Wan Li chaired the national urban economic restructuring conference. To his right are Tian Jiyun, Wang Zhaoguo and Song Ping

The Important Topic of Political Restructuring

Chen Yun and Deng Xiaoping, 1986

People's Daily published Wan Li's speech in full on 15 August 1986. The former vice premier, Tian Jiyun, said: "The speech is like a thundering alarm that has aroused a vehement response inside and outside the party."

Wan Li stressed that scientific and democratic decision-making had not received due attention, which was influenced by traditional values and was a reflection of the problems in China's political system. He cited an excessively centralised power structure and an incomplete decision-making system as two of the most serious problems in China's political system. "Even today, it is still common for leaders to make unchallenged decisions simply according to their experience. It is difficult to rectify wrong decisions and only when acute problems arise can they be rectified or redressed. By then, it will be too late. Now it's time for blind and hasty decision-making to be rectified. Otherwise, our socialist system would be incomplete and unsound, and China's economy would not be able to achieve constant and stable growth."

Deng Xiaoping, Hu Yaobang, Wan Li and others visit the Ming Tombs to plant trees, March 1983

Wan Li thought: "One important part of our political restructuring is to solve that problem. Only when decisions are made in a democratic and scientific manner can they complete and consolidate China's socialist system, carry forward hundreds of millions of Chinese people's sense of responsibility, give full scope to their enthusiasm and creativity, and consolidate the superiority of socialist systems."

Scientific and democratic decision-making is a permanent topic of modern decision-making and the primary focus of political restructuring. It is fundamental for democratic and scientific decision-making to avoid ruling by the voice of a single person but to handle affairs and rule the country according to scientific law. Political problems can be solved in a scientific and democratic way.

"Science and democracy are inseparable in a modern society," said Wan Li. "Without democracy, scientific development would be constrained. Without science, democracy would fail to become properly established. Similarly, scientific and democratic decision-making are inseparable. 'Scientific decision-making' largely depends on democratic decision-making. Without democracy, the wisdom of the people could not be pooled and there would be no encouragement for their views to be aired, let alone allowing respect for their knowledge, talent, wisdom, practical experience and science. In the same way, 'democratic decision-making' must be based on scientific meaning, procedure and methods. Otherwise, it would only be democracy in theory rather than in fact."

Commenting on the great significance of the speech, Comrade Tian Jiyun said: "To ensure democratic and scientific decision-making, Wan Li advocated adhering to the guideline of 'letting a hundred flowers bloom and a hundred schools of thought contend' to research policy and decision-making. That guideline should be the strategic policy that is unswervingly adopted in China's political life, ideological thinking and cultural construction. It is a pivotal sign of socialist democracy of a higher degree.

Wan Li said: "The guideline could not be implemented in the past because political issues were usually understood to be 'against the party', 'against socialism' and 'against revolution'. That concept caused huge side effects. As a matter of fact, on many occasions, academic issues and political issues could not be separated easily from each other."

He continued: "The key is not to separate academic issues from political issues but to apply the 'guideline' to both political issues and research on the decision-making of political issues. All political and policy issues should be researched and discussed, and contend with each other before a final decision is made. Different ideas and viewpoints should not 'be raised to a higher plane of principle and two-line struggle', 'besieged and criticised'. However, decisions must be made under certain principles or according to different circumstances.

Wan Li holds an informal discussion in Zhongnanhai with leading factory directors and managers from eight provinces and cities nationwide, listens to their ideas and vigorously supports and ardently encourages their spirit of accelerating the reform process, October 1984

In October 1985, the Chinese Academy of Social Sciences presented 131 scientists with a 'Certificate of honour for 50 Years of scientific work'. Here, Wan Li presents a certificate of honour to the famous scientist Mao Yisheng

"How could it be called 'highly democratic' if only the leaders and not the people were allowed to hold or air different views on political issues? I think we should encourage the free airing of views, lift censorship and implement free speech as stipulated in the Constitution. A big socialist power of one billion people featuring correct leadership, logical administration, harmony and booming economic development will not be crushed by any unpleasant political views or the instigation of people harbouring ulterior motives for whatever reason."

Wan Li's speech was made against the background of Comrade Deng Xiaoping repeatedly proposing the launch of political restructuring and it succeeded in provoking widespread discussion and capturing the attention of the whole of society and even the international community as well. In later reports of the 13th and 14th national congresses of the CPC, scientific and democratic decision-making was determined to be a vital topic to be solved during political restructuring.

Chapter 38

Accelerating Legislation in the Spirit of Reform

From 1 April 1988, China began to raise the purchase prices of some commodities such as grain, oil and sugar, relaxed the prices of major non-staple foods and implemented price reform. It was a far-reaching development for the country, the start of the dismantlement of the long-established planned economy.

Deng Xiaoping said that reform would succeed despite numerous difficulties: "Price reform must be implemented despite the risks and difficulties." Many potential problems arose and became prominent because of price reform and the whole nation discussed the issue.

Wan Li was elected chairman of the central committee at the first session of the seventh NPC in April 1988. He delivered a speech entitled 'To gradually establish the new order of the socialist commodity economy' at the second session of the NPC standing committee held on 1 July 1988.

The speech was aimed primarily at unifying the understanding of the standing committee and clearly defined its tasks. Wan Li fully affirmed the massive social changes brought about during the 10 years of reform and specifically analysed the prevailing problems. "These problems became acute not because of the reforms themselves but because they were not implemented completely and the old institutions still enabled these problems to persist," he said. "Take the hike in prices as an example. In addition to an excessively rapid rise in social demand that resulted in supply-demand conflicts, another fundamental reason for the creation of such conflicts and the rise in prices was that we had to simultaneously allow planned prices and market prices. The binary price system did play a positive role during the transition period of China's price reform. However, with the further development of the market economy, its defects were more apparent because it did not conform to the requirements of the law of value, did not benefit both producers and consumers, and did not help to guarantee clean governance. Various illegal and immoral phenomena, such as illegally reselling commodities at a profit, feathering one's own nest, bribery, corruption and unfair social phenomena, were all connected with it to some degree. The crux of the problem was that the old system remained partially intact and the new system had not been completely established."

Newly-elected Chairman Wan Li of the NPC standing committee shows his respect to Chairman Peng Zhen of the sixth NPC standing committee, 1988

Deng Xiaoping, Peng Zhen and Wan Li talk during a break in the first session of the seventh NPC, March 1988

Wan Li hosts the opening ceremony of the seventh NPC

Wan Li hosts the 15th session of the NPC standing committee that passed the *Copyright Law of the PRC*, **the** *Railway Law of the PRC* **and the** *Law of the PRC on the Protection of The Rights and Interests of Returned Overseas Chinese and the Family Members of Overseas Chinese*, **September 1990**

The third session of the seventh NPC passed the Basic Law of Hong Kong SAR of the PRC. Wan Li chairs the session

The first session of the seventh NPC closed in April 1988. The session passed the *Law of the PRC on Industrial Enterprises Owned by the Whole People*, the *Law of the PRC on Sino-Foreign Contracted Joint Ventures* and the *Amendment to the Constitution of the PRC*. According to the amendment, Article 11 of the constitution should include a new paragraph that read: 'The state permits the private sector of the economy to exist and develop within the limits prescribed by law. The private sector of the economy is a complement to the socialist public economy.' Here, representatives vote by a show of hands and pass the resolution

After analysing the advantages of reform, Wan Li said: "What is the crucial stage of reform? It is a period of breakthrough featuring both great risks and great opportunities. If suspicion and mistrust prevail and we miss the opportunity, the road ahead will be rugged; if we take resolute decisions and make a breakthrough, the road ahead will be smooth. We must brave the storm and move on; if we retreat, we will find ourselves in a blind alley."

In accordance with China's circumstances and the tasks of reform, Wan Li proposed that the NPC standing committee must focus on the following work: accelerate legislation and the establishment of the new order of the market economy; unite with people of all nationalities to support the reform and overcome the difficulties; enhance democratic and legal construction, and consolidate and develop a stable and united political situation.

Wan Li and Qiao Shi attend the national government legal work conference, 28 April 1987

To accelerate legislation in the spirit of reform became the central task of the seventh NPC.

Legislation and reform should proceed simultaneously and urgently needed laws should be formulated as soon as possible. To expedite the legislation, Wan Li said: "We can refer to the mature laws on the market economies of foreign countries and Hong Kong and absorb those aspects that are suitable for China so that we don't have to start from scratch."

In December 1988, the NPC established a five-year legislative plan and focused on researching and formulating laws relating to governing the economic environment and rectifying the economic order over the following two years. Vice Chairman Peng Chong held a meeting to draft the Initial Deployment to Accelerate Legislation in the Next Two Years and put forward specific measures to speed up legislation.

Deng Xiaoping and Wan Li shake hands, 19 October 1992

After Deng Xiaoping made a speech during his southern inspection tour in 1992, Wan Li delivered an important speech at the 26th session of the seventh NPC. "How should the market economy be controlled after it is established?" he asked. "First, it should be legalised and laws should be applied to control the private economy and foreign-funded enterprises. At the same time, we should give full play to the banks and make use of flexible fiscal and financial measures concerning interest rates, tax rates and the exchange rate to control the economy. Guaranteeing the smooth development of the socialist market economy in a legal manner became an important task for the NPC, the NPC standing committee, the local people's congresses and their standing committees."

At that meeting, legislative power was officially conferred to Shenzhen municipality. Wan Li said: "I think it is right to confer legislative power to Shenzhen because it will stimulate the development of the socialist market economy and promote reform and opening up as well as democratic and legal construction."

Under the direction of Wan Li, the standing committee of the seventh NPC successively formulated laws that had an important influence on China's economic construction and reform and opening up, such as the *Law of the PRC on Industrial Enterprises Owned by the Whole People*, the *Law of the PRC on Sino-Foreign Contracted Joint Ventures*, the *Income Tax Law of the PRC for Enterprises with Foreign Investment and Foreign Enterprises*, the *Maritime Law*, the *Law of the PRC on the Administration of Tax Collection* and the *Product Quality Law*, summarised the latest economic developments and reform and opening up, modified and improved the Land Management Law, the Environmental Protection Act, the Patent Law and the Trademark Act and reviewed drafts of the *Corporation Law, the Agriculture Law and the Scientific and Technological Progress Law of the PRC*.

Jiang Zemin, Yang Shangkun and Wan Li talk cordially during the first general assembly of the third session of the seventh NPC, 21 March 1990

At the same time, the NPC standing committee prioritised the formulation of law protecting personal rights and made a series of laws and acts such as the *Trade Union Law*, the *Administrative Procedure Law*, the *Copyright Law*, the *Law of the PRC on the Protection of Rights and Interests of Women* and the *Law of the PRC on Protection of Disabled Persons*. It also formulated the *Basic Law of Hong Kong SAR* and submitted the *Basic Law of the Macau SAR* to the congress for review.

The seventh NPC and its standing committee passed a total of 59 laws and 27 decisions on legal problems in addition to an amendment. More legislation was passed by the NPC than at any other time in that period.

Chapter 39

Suggesting a Modification to the 1982 Constitution

Wan Li was no longer a central committee member or a member of the political bureau of the central committee at the time of the 14th national congress of the CPC and the first plenary session of the 14th central committee of the CPC held in October 1992, while the standing committee of the seventh NPC would expire in March 1993. This meant that, due to his advancing years, Wan Li would retreat from Chinese politics.

After the 14th national congress of the CPC, Wan Li referred to *The Constitution*, repeatedly read the documents of the 14th national congress of the CPC and believed some major issues in *The Constitution* must be modified. At a party group meeting of the NPC standing committee on 28 October 1992, Wan Li said six issues needed to be modified:

1. Deng Xiaoping's theory on building socialism with Chinese characteristics is the guiding ideology of the CPC. The basic party line should not be changed in 100 years. But the prevailing constitution neither explained that theory nor the basic party line. Such a statement should be expressly mentioned in the foreword or in the general principles of the constitution.
2. Persisting in reform and opening up is a component of the party's basic line. For 10 years, the Chinese people have benefited considerably from reform and opening up. How can the constitution not mention reform and opening up? 'Persisting in reform and opening up' must be added to the foreword or to the general principles of the constitution.
3. The practice of implementing a market economy has gone ahead. Since the third plenary session of the 11th central committee of the CPC, Guangzhou, Shenzhen and other places have implemented a

market economy and developed reasonably well. The 14th national congress of the CPC decided to establish a socialist market economy system and elaborated on it theoretically. But the prevailing constitution stipulates the implementation of a planned economy. So, the constitution must be modified without delay. The constitution should clearly stipulate that the state should implement a socialist market economy. Otherwise, implementing the market economy is equivalent to violating the constitution.

Wan Li chairs the fifth session of the seventh NPC, March 1992

Wan Li and Qiao Shi attend a meeting to celebrate the 10th anniversary of the promulgation of *The Constitution of the PRC*, December 1992

4. Consideration should be made to include in the constitution the standards of developing socialist productivity, enhancing the overall strength of a socialist country and improving people's lives proposed by Deng Xiaoping.
5. The constitution should stipulate that the rural contracted responsibility system should not be changed in the long term. The phrase 'people's commune' in the constitution should be deleted.
6. The party constitution has increased the term of office of the county party committee from three years to five years and the constitution should also increase the term of the county government and the county people's congress from three years to five years.

Wan Li proposed to set up a constitution modification team; submit to the CPC central committee the report on the modification of the constitution; and take a positive attitude, quicken the work and strive to pass the amendment of the constitution at the first session of the eighth NPC under the leadership of the central committee.

Subsequently, the constitution modification team was set up and the amendment of the constitution was formulated. Most of Wan Li's proposals were adopted and the constitution was modified accordingly. The amendment of the constitution was passed and declared to be implemented at the first session of the eighth NPC on 29 March 1993.

Chapter 40

Not Inquiring into Matters, Running Affairs or Stirring up Trouble

The NPC's new five-year term started in March 1993 and Wan Li was relieved of his post as chairman of the standing committee of the seventh NPC. After the handover in the Great Hall of the People, Wan Li warmly hugged Comrade Qiao Shi, his successor as chairman of the NPC, and bid farewell to politics. That scene touched all the people around.

Wan Li and the newly elected Chairman Qiao Shi of the standing committee of the eighth NPC hug each other at the first session of the eighth NPC, March 1993

On returning to his home in Hanhetang in Zhongnanhai, Wan Li sat in a sofa in his parlour and asked his private secretary to turn on all the lights in the room. Asking his wife Bian Tao to sit nearby, he talked with his children and his private secretary.

"Today, I managed to retire safe and sound," he said. "I will now spend my remaining years in comfort. Then, I will take steps to arrange for my death. It is my 'three safety' policy. From tomorrow onwards, I will live the life of an ordinary person. You can buy me a cotton-padded jacket with cloth buttons down the front and a pair of hand-made cloth shoes from Neiliansheng [a famous shoe store in China]. The western-style clothes and the leather shoes can be put aside because I won't wear them."

At the closing ceremony of the first session of the eighth NPC in March 1993, Wan Li stands up, acknowledges the representatives and bids farewell to politics amid thunderous applause

A married couple very much in love — retired Wan Li and Bian Tao in the garden of their home in Zhongnanhai

All those present said euthanasia was not auspicious and should be avoided. His response was straightforward: "Auspicious or not, the objective law of nature is ruthless and everyone has to face death in the end. We are CPC members and should treat it from the perspective of historical materialism."

Afterwards, he said solemnly: "In future, I will have 'three nots': not to participate in any official activities; not to take any honorary posts and cancel all my current positions [11 at the time], leaving only the posts of honorary chairman of the Chinese Bridge Association and the Chinese Tennis Association; and not to write any inscriptions."

Two days later, he asked the director of the central guard bureau, Yang Dezhong, to his house. "I have retired," he told him. "It will be fine to leave just one of my two guards and cancel the security vehicle. The central guard bureau and the public security guard should not send anyone to accompany me when I go to play tennis, play bridge or have meals."

Deep love between grandfather and granddaughter — Wan Zhenyang kisses Wan Li

Afterwards, the central guard bureau held a meeting to discuss the situation and finally decided to respect Wan Li's suggestion. When he moved about in central Beijing, it would be sufficient to make a record in the duty room of the central guard bureau.

Wan Li wrote a poem at this time: "No worries after retirement, / it's fun to play bridge and tennis / together with good friends; / if the country is prosperous and the people live in peace, / I can enjoy my later years in contentment."

After the third session of the fifth NPC, the state gradually established a set of complete retirement systems that had been initially implemented. When Wan Li retired, they were still getting to grips with how the old cadres spent their twilight years. The poem spread far and wide, was cited by newspapers and created strong reverberations at home and abroad.

Soon after he retired, Wan Li was invited to join the organising committee of the seventh national sports competition in Beijing as they deliberated the grand opening in September 1993. He and some of his friends came to view the stadium in Pinggu village, in a mountainous area in Beijing's suburbs. Soon afterwards, the publication launch of the *Selected Works of Deng Xiaoping* and the celebration rally at the 100th anniversary of Mao Zedong's birth were grand occasions held in the capital city, but Wan Li was not in attendance.

Many people were baffled by his absence and came up with different explanations. In the spring festival of 1994, Wan Li decided to clarify his thinking: "Past leaders can participate in some activities. But we cannot say that those who do not participate are dissenting in some way, or are not supportive. Leaders should organise activities in a practical and realistic manner and try their utmost to reduce or avoid nepotism; participants should be well motivated and avoid appearing just for the sake of it."

Wan Li handled such problems on the principle of 'not interfering, running affairs or stirring up trouble', in other words, not inquiring into matters that didn't concern him; not running affairs that were not his business; and not making trouble. Wan Li thought it was the best way to

Wan Li and Bian Tao with their son, daughter-in-law and granddaughters in Hanhetang in Zhongnanhai

support the new leaders. He said: "The 'three nots' do not mean that I do not care for the events of the party and the state. I will give my candid answers, views and suggestions to the leaders if they would like to hear them. But my answers should only serve as a reference. Without doubt, I will also air my opinion when I think it is necessary."

The 45th anniversary of the founding of the PRC was celebrated in 1994 with a large fireworks display in Beijing. Wan Li refused to attend. His staff members and children felt anxious. Wan Li fully understood their anxiety and said it was not necessary to watch the fireworks from Tiananmen gate tower since they could watch them from elsewhere.

After retirement, Wan Li missed his hometown greatly and showed great interest in Dongping's development and construction. Here, Jin Zhaohong, secretary of Dongping county's Zhoucheng Street working committee, shows Wan Li the brilliant vision of the old county restoration plan

Wan Li and Bian Tao pictured with their five children in a Tianjin guesthouse. Back row from left: third son Wan Jifei, second son Wan Zhongxiang, eldest son Wan Boao, daughter Wan Shupeng and youngest son Wan Xiaowu

Wan Li fishing

Jiang Zemin and Liu Huaqing pay a new year visit to the home of Wan Li, 7 February 1994

Comrade Xi Jinping pays a visit to Comrade Wan Li, 1 February 2013

On the evening of 1 October, he and his family and friends gathered to watch the fireworks in the Tibet Room, located in the northeastern corner on the third floor of the Great Hall of the People. Wan Li said: "Isn't this a good place to watch the fireworks!"

The next day, the newspapers and television announced a long list of participating leaders and retired leaders, Wan Li's name not included. Wan Li said: "We came to watch the fireworks rather than make an appearance. It doesn't matter whether the names of the retirees appear in the list or not."

Chapter 41

Honorary Chairman of the Chinese Bridge and Tennis Associations

After his retirement, Wan Li decided to continue with just two of his honorary posts — honorary chairman of the Chinese Tennis Association and the Chinese Bridge Association.

Wan Li loved exercise and sports. On retirement, he said: "I hope to have 'three no trumps' when I play bridge and to die on the bridge table." His deep love for bridge startled his family.

Wan Li's life was far from boring after retirement. He had a regular routine. Each day, he would take a nap after lunch and, after getting up at 3pm, participate in sport. Every week he played bridge three times, tennis four times and golf once.

Wan Li often said: "I can play tennis, which means I'm physically sound. I can play bridge, which means I'm mentally sound." He learnt to play tennis as a teenager when he studied at Qufu normal school in Shandong and began to learn to play bridge when he and Comrade Xiaoping liberated southwestern China and left Nanjing for Chongqing by boat during the war of liberation. He learnt from experienced bridge players and soon became skilled. Later, he became a bridge partner of Comrade Xiaoping. From then on, however busy he might be, he would spare time for the two activities. Bridge and tennis were his lifelong passions. Apart from during wartime, he was a regular bridge and tennis player, even during the 10 tough and chaotic years.

At the first representative conference of the Chinese Bridge Association, Wan Li made a speech in his capacity of honorary chairman, earnestly requesting that all managerial staff of the association and all fans of bridge nationwide could strive to popularise and enhance the game in China. "The

Chinese people are smart and can probably improve the level of bridge," he said. "I hope Chinese bridge players can give full scope to their talent and wisdom, and endeavour to make China a world bridge power at the 20th anniversary of the establishment of the Chinese Bridge Association." It became the objective for the development of bridge in China.

Even in old age, Wan Li remained vigorous and hearty

Honorary Chairman of the Chinese Bridge and Tennis Associations

In November 2005, Wan Li celebrated 75 years of playing tennis at Xiannongtan tennis court in Beijing. Far left is Bai Jie, chairman of the Beijing Veteran Tennis Association

92-year-old Wan Li remains active on the tennis court

Wan Li executes a classic forehand drive on the tennis court

Wan Li plays bridge to keep his mind active after retirement

Wan Li was a good bridge player. In 1984, he partnered Ms Yang Xiaoyan, an American-Chinese and world-famous bridge player to win the game's most prestigious prize, the Solomon Prize. This was a prize presented to the world's best-played hand of the year. The editor of the *New York Times* bridge column commented: "The southern player [Wan Li] fully showed his daring spirit and extraordinary courage and insight by doubling the final call. Chinese leaders tend to double their efforts to make progress, which foreign diplomatic officers must bear in mind."

Wan Li also once won second place in the Epson world bridge pairs. Yang Xiaoyan once commented in a magazine that a grand slam game performance of Wan Li showed his vigour and courage and displayed the qualities of a statesman.

Wan Li participated in many friendly events, invitation tournaments and regular championships. He played with many people, including government officials, journalists, undergraduates and workers. He scored many outstanding achievements due to his wisdom and high skill level.

Wan Li was seldom late for tennis or bridge. However, on one occasion, he overslept until noon. He dressed quickly and said: "Hurry, hurry! I'm late!" Some people thought that something serious must have happened.

Honorary Chairman of the Chinese Bridge and Tennis Associations

Wan Li, Deng Xiaoping, Hu Yaobang and Ding Guangen participate in an invitation competition among old comrades

Wan Li presents the trophy of the ninth 'strategy and wealth' bridge competition to Deng Xiaoping

On seeing his fellow bridge players, he apologised again and again: "I'm late. Sorry for having kept you waiting." He then went on to play with an easy grace, as was his custom.

He told his family many times that bridge was a noble, civilised game that would significantly benefit their health, minds and even careers, throughout their lives. He often said that bridge fans were generally good at evaluation and self-criticism because the level of bridge playing could be constantly enhanced and that cooperation and coordination among both players could become more tacit only when they had learnt from their mistakes and changed their way of thinking rather than attributing any failures to their partners. Only in that way can both players make progress.

When Wan Li heard that someone could play bridge or tennis, his eyes would shine. He seldom communicated with non-family members in his daily life except with fellow bridge players. He rarely talked about family

Wan Li, honorary chairman of the Chinese Bridge Association, meets Chinese and foreign players participating in the 'Friendship Cup' international bridge invitation competition in Beijing's Great Hall of the People, June 1989. Here, Wan Li chats with American bridge player Yang Xiaoyan (centre), known as the 'Queen of Bridge'

Honorary Chairman of the Chinese Bridge and Tennis Associations

Wan Li receives the 'Eagle Brand American Ginseng Cup' bridge competition trophy, March 1992

Liu Huaqing watches Wan Li play bridge

Wan Li and the chairman of the Chinese Tennis Association, Lǚ Zhengcao, chat with children, May 1984

The chairman of the International Olympic Committee, Antonio Samaranch, presents an Olympic gold pendant to Wan Li in the Great Hall of the People to commend his special contributions to the Olympic Games and Chinese sport in general, April 1986

life but he did that with his fellow bridge players and even chatted about their family lives, too.

When he played bridge, Wan Li often revealed his true sentiments. If he felt happy, during a break, he would sing old songs such as *In Praise of the Red Plum, 18 September* and *Return from the Shooting Range*. His fellow players would clap their hands and sing together with him excitedly. The cultural atmosphere of bridge created a special bond between fellow players.

The chairman of the World Bridge Federation once lavished praise on Wan Li: "Wan Li is a bridge lover full of vitality. He is known for his wisdom and far-sightedness, enjoying a good reputation in international and Chinese bridge circles, and in other aspects. As a bridge lover and a state leader, Wan Li's meticulous guidance for and active participation in bridge in China will have a huge influence and encourage more bridge lovers.

"Wan Li is the best bridge player among state leaders. It is in promoting the welfare of Chinese bridge circles that Wan Li acts as honorary chairman of the Chinese Bridge Association."

Chapter 42

Still Keeping a Watchful Eye on Socialist Legal Construction

Retired, Wan Li still clung to his longstanding habit of reading newspapers and magazines. After supper each evening, he would watch television, one of his major sources of information. He particularly liked watching news programmes and Beijing opera.

In addition to reading books and newspapers, he also put aside an hour to meet visitors. Central committee and provincial party committee leaders, old comrades-in-arms, former colleagues, friends, fellow tennis and bridge players, writers and journalists came to see him in an endless stream. He also welcomed and received cadres and farmers who came to see him from rural areas, including representatives from Xiaogang village. He would talk with them for a fairly long time and, when they departed, he would escort them in person to the gate.

Wan Li and Bian Tao in Zhongnanhai

Wan Li still paid attention to the development of reform and opening up and thought about the construction of the market economy, democracy and the legal system. He paid close attention to

Retired, Wan Li still kept a watchful eye on socialist legal construction

agriculture and systematically reviewed the process of rural reform.

Yu Zuomin, the president of Agriculture, Industry and Commerce Corporation in Daqiu village, Jinghai county, Tianjin, was an influential man in China's reform process. He was placed in criminal detention according to the law in April 1993 and was sentenced to 20 years in prison on 27 August.

On 20 April, five days after his arrest, Wan Li talked with senior figures at *Economic Daily* and *Legal Daily*. Wan Li thought that the Daiqiuzhuang incident "posed a very acute and serious problem to the Chinese authorities and the Chinese people: how to establish and complete the legal system in reform and opening up. Without such a system, China's order would sooner or later become chaotic and the cause of reform and opening up would be thoroughly destroyed.

"The symbol of a modernised country is not only economic prosperity. For instance, some rich countries are feudal autocracies and they cannot be regarded as modernised. It is because of the lack of democracy and the legal system in some parts of China that Yu Zuomin and others had nothing to fear and violated the law and public opinion. It was a typical case. Such social phenomena did not appear by accident. Widespread instances of bribery and the abuse of power for personal gain constituted one of the important reasons to take action. It was a reflection of a feudal society and brought serious harm to socialism. Without democracy and the legal system, the development of township enterprises would lead to illegality and criminality."

Wan Li regarded the Daqiuzhuang incident as 'valuable treasure' from which profound democratic and legal lessons could be learned. The incident alerted "the whole party and the whole nation to the fact that we must accelerate our progress towards establishing and improving a legal society and a market economy on a legal basis. The legal system should be applied to guarantee the operation of the market mechanism so as to strengthen the legal concept of the whole party and the whole people, and so that the concept of modernisation can move ahead for the entire nation.

"China should make long-term efforts to become a highly legalised society. At the moment, it is still very common for people to be unaware

Wan Li presents the letter of appointment to Ma Wanqi, deputy director of the drafting committee of the Basic Law of Macau SAR, October 1988

Hu Jintao pays a visit to Wan Li, 2007

of prevailing laws, and for laws to be broken and for lawbreakers to escape punishment. There are too many feudal remnants in China. As a consequence, efforts should be made to publicise the legal system, criticise illegal practice and establish the quintessence of legal system implementation."

Wan Li concluded: "Without high democracy and the legal system, China cannot modernise. Apart from economic development, the legal system is an indispensable element of modernisation. It won't do simply to make policies; what is required is an upgrade of the party's policies and laws. It is a major task for China to fully understand and attach importance to the socialist market economy. We should mobilise the enthusiasm and creativity of our people and implement the market economy in the course of China's economic construction. In implementing the market economy, we must guarantee that producers and operators are able to decide for themselves, have their own freedoms and enjoy democracy that should be standardised and guaranteed by the socialist legal system. For this reason, the market economy is the legal economy in a certain sense."

Li Keqiang visits Wan Li in his home in Zhongnanhai

Wan Li attached high priority to legal system construction. His view that "the market economy is the legal economy" remains of great significance for guiding China's socialist modernisation.

Epilogue

During the spring festival of 2002, Wan Li travelled to Guangdong in the company of his eldest son, Wan Boao. It was to be his last long journey. He wanted to bid farewell to the people of Guangdong who were at the forefront of reform and opening up.

During the spring festival of 2002, Wan Li paid a visit to Shenzhen and to Xi Zhongxun's house. The two old comrades-in-arms chat amiably

Wan Li and Ren Zhongyi shake hands and talk cordially

While in Guangdong, Wan Li paid a special visit to two people. One was Xi Zhongxun, who was seriously ill at that time. During the spring festival, Xi Zhongxun Xi was wearing red to demonstrate his great joy at the prospect of meeting Wan Li. They excitedly embraced one other when they met.

Wan Li said: "I have come to see my old companion." Xi Zhongxun corrected him: "No, not old companions but old comrades-in-arms." They talked happily and enjoyed a good time.

The other person Wan Li went to see, in the company of Comrade Li Changchun, was Ren Zhongyi, another senior general of reform and opening up. They were old acquaintances.

After that, Wan Li stayed at home in Beijing and spent his final years quietly and happily.

Comrade Wan Li died of an illness in Beijing on 15 July 2015 at the age of 99.

Epilogue

People's Daily announced Wan Li's death on its front page, stating: 'The CPC central committee, the standing committee of the NPC, the state council and the CPPCC hereby sadly announce the death of Comrade Wan Li'

万里同志遗体在京火化
习近平等到八宝山革命公墓送别

The site of the farewell ceremony for Comrade Wan Li

Wan Li's body is placed among flowers and cypress plants, covered with the bright red flag of the CPC

Chronology

December 1916
Born in Dongping county, Shandong province
1936
Joined the CPC
After 1937
Appointed secretary of the CPC Dongping county work committee and director of the CPC's Taixi prefectural committee publicity department and organisation department
After 1940
Appointed deputy director of the CPC western Shandong committee and the second, seventh and eighth secretary of the CPC Hebei-Shandong-Henan prefectural committee
1947
Appointed member and secretary of the CPC Hebei-Shandong-Henan prefectural committee
April 1949
Appointed deputy director of the accounting and finance committee, director of the economy department and director of the construction bureau of the military control committee
June 1950
Appointed member of the accounting, economy and finance committee of the southwestern military and administrative commission, deputy director and then director of the industrial department of the southwestern military and administrative commission

November 1952

Appointed standing deputy director of the department of building engineering of the CPC central committee

April 1955

Appointed director of the state council's state administration of urban construction

May 1956

Appointed director of the urban construction department

1958

Appointed secretary of the secretariat of the CPC Beijing municipal committee and deputy mayor of Beijing

After September 1959

Appointed vice chairman of the second, third and fourth Beijing municipal people's political consultative conference

May 1973

Appointed secretary of the CPC Beijing municipal committee and deputy director of the revolutionary committee

January 1975

Appointed minister of railways

1976

Appointed first deputy director of the department of light industry

June 1977

Appointed first secretary of the CPC Anhui provincial committee

January 1978

Appointed director of the revolutionary committee and first political commissar of Anhui provincial military region

February 1980

Elected secretary of the secretariat of the central committee at the fifth plenary session of the 11th central committee of the CPC

April 1980

Elected vice premier of the state council

August 1980

Appointed director of the national agricultural council

December 1980
Selected as honorary chairman of the Chinese Bridge Association

September 1982
Elected as a member of the political bureau of the central committee at the first plenary session of the 12th central committee of the CPC

1982
Elected co-chairman of the central afforestation committee and honorary chairman of the Chinese Tennis Association

1984
Elected honorary chairman of the Chinese society for urban studies

November 1987
Elected member of the political bureau of the central committee at the first plenary session of the 13th central committee of the CPC

April 1988
Elected chairman of the standing committee of the seventh NPC

1990
Elected honorary chairman of the China Green Foundation

March 1993
Retired from leading positions

April 1993
Elected honorary president of the China Environmental Protection Foundation

June 1993
Awarded a gold pendant from the IOC for his contributions to the Olympic Games and sport in China

1995
Re-elected as third honorary chairman of the China Green Foundation

15 July 2015
Died of illness in Beijing at the age of 99